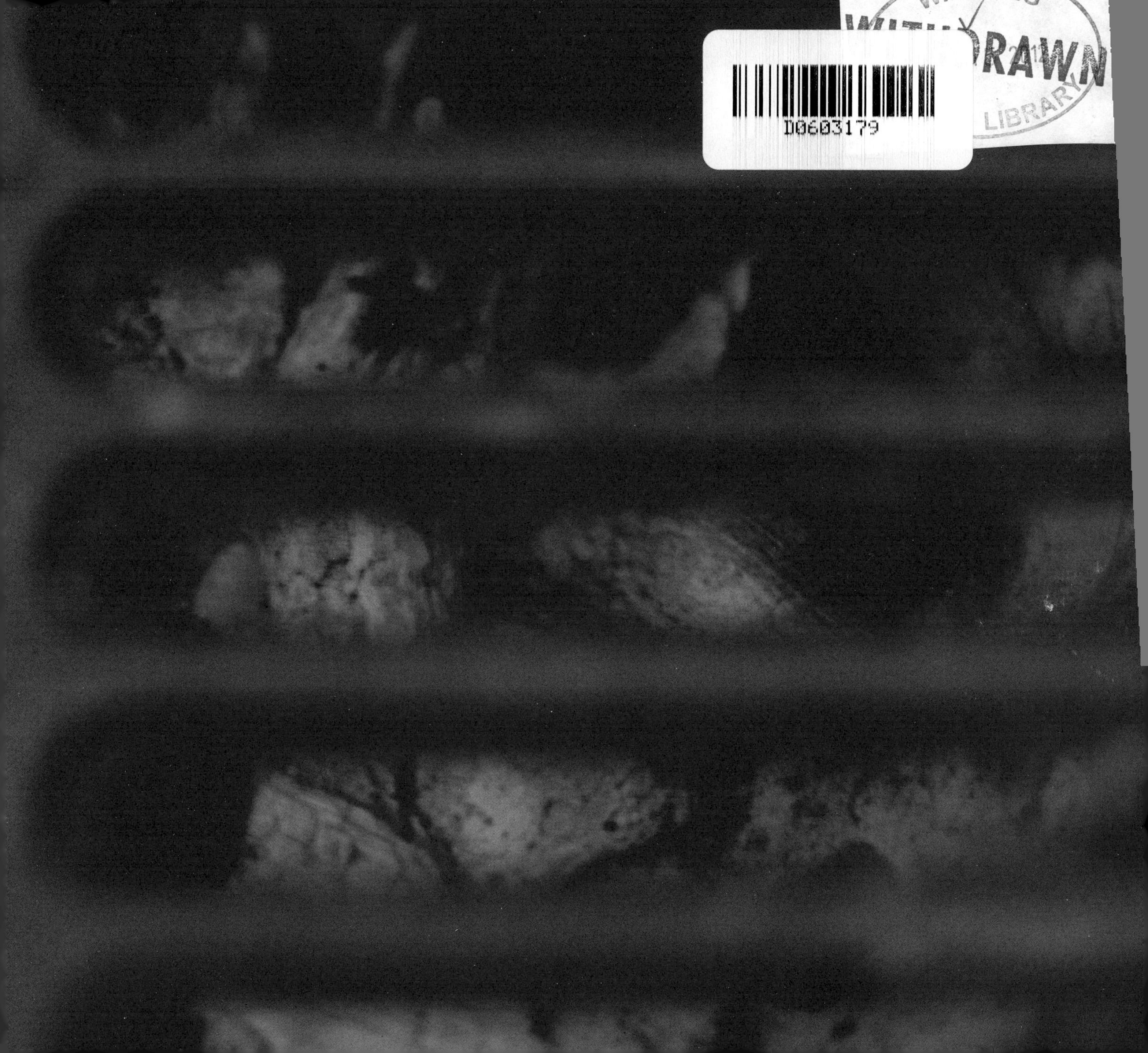

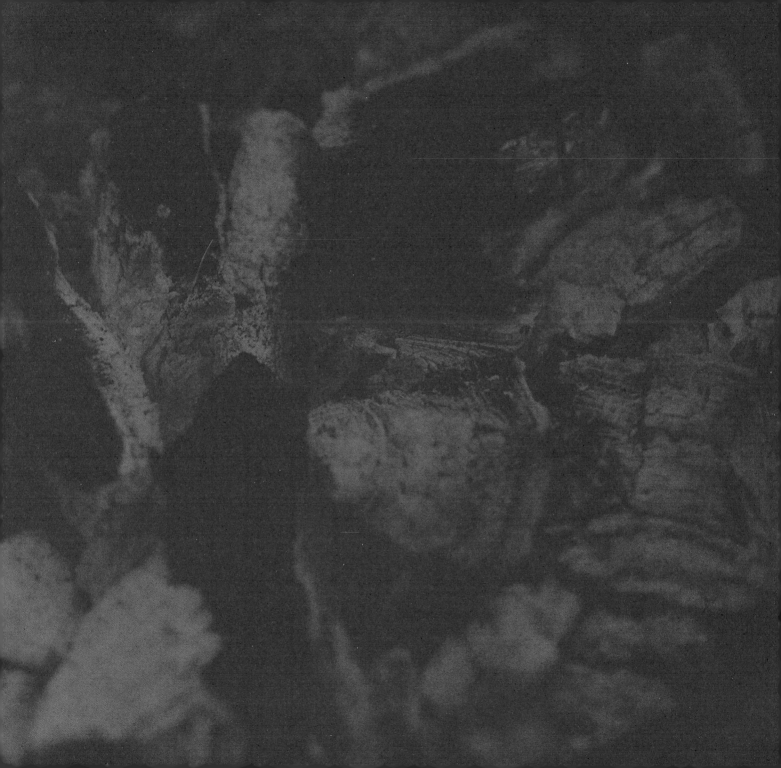

SLOW FIRE

THE BEGINNER'S GUIDE TO BARBECUE

BY RAY "DR. BBQ" LAMPE
FOREWORD BY FAMOUS DAVE ANDERSON
PHOTOGRAPHS BY LEIGH BEISCH

CHRONICLE BOOKS
SAN FRANCISCO

THANKS

to Bruce Romanek for starting it all that day in Grant Park so long ago. Thanks to Dave Dewitt for starting my career in writing. Thanks to Scott Mendel for always putting me in the right place. Thanks to Bill LeBlond for always having faith in me. Thanks to Leigh Beisch for the great photos. Thanks to Tim Bryan for bringing the smoke! Thanks to Alice Chau for making it all look good. Thanks to my parents for giving me the tools. Thanks to Marsha for another great recipe. Thanks to Sandi for putting up with me while I write.

Text copyright © 2012 by Ray Lampe.
Photographs copyright © 2012 by Leigh Beisch.

Library of Congress Cataloging-in-Publication Data available.
ISBN 978-1-4521-0303-7

Manufactured in China.

Designed by Alice Chau
Typesetting by DC Typography
Prop styling by Christine Wolheim
Food styling by Robyn Valarik
The photographer wishes to thank Tim Bryan of Greenleaf BBQ; Michael Melby, Scott Johnston, and Dustin Clausen of Starvin' Marvin's Bay Area BBQ; Weber; and Ray for inclusion on another great project.

10 9 8 7 6 5 4 3 2 1

Chronicle Books LLC
680 Second Street
San Francisco, California 94107
www.chroniclebooks.com

This book is
dedicated to

SANDI

xxoo

CONTENTS

FOREWORD

IF YOU ARE A PORK-AHOLIC LOOKING FOR A RIB-O-LICIOUSLY GOOD RECIPE . . . THIS IS THE COOKBOOK THAT'S GUARANTEED TO GIVE YOU A MOUTHFUL OF HOLLERS!

Hi! This is "Famous Dave" Anderson, founder of Famous Dave's Bar-B-Que and one of America's most passionate lovers of anything smoky, charred, grilled, or slathered with secret concoctions of magical herbs, spices, and fruit juices and slow-smoked over smoldering embers. I am a steadfast believer that man has a primal craving for chewing charred meat off a bone. It just brings out his inner caveman, and there is no question that Ray Lampe has to be King of the Molten Sauces and Smoked Meats.

For forty years, I have been on a personal quest to discover the holy grail of barbecue—the trinity of meat, smoke, and sauce. In the beginning, back when charcoal was just beginning to be squeezed into briquettes, I can remember saving up enough money to buy my first barbecue cookbook from Sunset Publishing. Their idea of a barbecue sauce was nothing more than ketchup, brown sugar, and Worcestershire sauce. I knew from my dad, an old Choctaw Indian from the Bible Belt of Oklahoma, that there was more to great-tasting barbecue sauce and smoked meats than I was going to find in a cook book. The only way you were going to really learn the craft of award-winning barbecue was if you were able to find some old-time pitmaster from the Deep South who was willing to fess up his hard-earned secrets. And the reality of this happening was next to impossible.

Until now, that is! Meet Ray Lampe— or Dr. BBQ—the closest thing you'll ever get to a real old-time championship pitmaster. To say that Ray Lampe loves barbecue would be an understatement. Ray Lampe is the self-professed Don King of Barbecue, with his hair sticking straight up and clothes all aflame. Ray is a tireless promoter of all things smoky, sticky, and addictive. For over thirty years, Dr. BBQ has devoted himself to eating, drinking, and sleeping *BARBECUE*. All you have to do is take one look at Ray and you can tell this man eats for a living! Unlike the old pitmasters who never gave up their closely guarded secrets, Ray is passionate about spreading the gospel of barbecue.

In this book, *Slow Fire*, Ray spills the beans on how to turn your backyard grill into the best rib joint in town! Dr. BBQ reveals all the pitmaster secrets to mixing up your own secret rubs and sauces and how to smoke meats slow and low over glowing embers until they are mouth-wateringly tender and juicy. *Slow Fire* is the real deal. There are no namby-pamby *Good Housekeeping*–type recipes in this book! When followed with the same passion as they were written, every one of these award-winning recipes will knock the socks off your family and friends. Some of my personal *Slow Fire* favorites are Dr. BBQ's Smoky Braised Beef Short Ribs (page 68) served up with a sassy side of Cheesy Jalapeño Grits (page 165). The robustly flavorful Cuban-Style Leg of Pork (page 79) will have you thinking that your taste buds just took a vacation to South Miami! Once you start cooking out of Dr. BBQ's *Slow Fire* cookbook, you'll never go back to cooking on a gas stove again! *Enjoy. . . .*

"MAY YOU ALWAYS BE SURROUNDED BY GOOD FRIENDS AND GREAT-TASTING BARBECUE!"

Rib-O-Liciously Yours,
"Famous Dave" Anderson

THE ART OF BARBECUE

There is something magical about barbecue that makes it different from any other cuisine. No matter where my travels take me, there is always a local barbecue joint that is known far and wide as the best there is and the people who cook there are revered. They've even been given a title that sets them apart from any other cook in the kitchen: The Pitmaster. And a pitmaster's secrets are accepted as something only he knows. He's a sorcerer of sauce and a wizard of wood.

Cooking great barbecue is unique and mysterious and we all love to eat it. Just about every carnivore I've ever met can tell you where to find the best barbecue he ever had. But for many new barbecue cooks, the idea that they could re-create this wonderful cuisine at home seems pretty far-fetched. They see the big concrete block barbecue pits built into the walls of restaurants or the big shiny industrial smokers on trailers outside and they can't imagine where they'd even start. I was one of those guys twenty-some years ago, but I wasn't willing to accept that this cooking method was only for the big boys. There had to be a way for the beginner to create good and authentic barbecue at home.

I've spent a lot of time since then learning the ways of the legends. I've been lucky enough to travel to all of the lower forty-eight in my pursuit of barbecue knowledge and I've seen everything. I've eaten in most of the shrines that have been serving barbecue for decades and I've talked to the pitmasters who cook it. I've competed on the national barbecue cook-off circuit at a high level for a couple of decades and I count the top champions of all time as my friends. I've even written a few cookbooks on the subject. I've worked for grill companies and even a famous barbecue restaurant, and I've cooked on just about every type of smoker or grill that you could imagine. I know how the equipment works and I know how the barbecue is created. It's created with meat and fire. It's the original cooking method. What could have come before that and what could be more simple?

Modern-day barbecue is a little more refined, but I've spent hundreds of hours breaking it down and teaching people so that even the greenest beginner can do it. The old tradition of barbecue is to take the lesser cuts of meat and cook them slowly over a wood fire until they become tender and delicious. That's the basic principle and when you do that, magical things begin to happen. It's kind of like making a roux in Louisiana-style cooking, where the flavor develops over time and it just can't be rushed. The long, slow cooking with spices and wood smoke added for flavor helps to develop the deep mahogany-colored outside crust we lovingly call the "bark" into an intensely flavored shell that is what the taste of real barbecue is all about. At the same time, the "inside meat" is slowly cooking into mouth-watering tenderness and rendering the excess fat. This can happen only with cuts of meat that are tough to begin with and loaded with collagen. As the collagen breaks down it enhances the taste of the meat but it also creates that mouthfeel that covers your tongue with creamy goodness. The end result is a mix of the amazing flavor of the outside crust combined with the juicy, tender, velvety meat from the inside and the combination is about the best thing you'll ever eat. This all may sound complicated, but I'm here to tell you that you can create this kind of great barbecue at home and you don't need the skills of a Master Chef to do it. With a small investment in a home smoker and a little practice, you will go from beginner to the champion of your neighborhood in no time.

To get started cooking real barbecue, the only equipment a beginner really needs is a closed grill or smoker capable of cooking at low consistent temps. There are a lot of affordable ways to do this and you should have no problem finding one to fit your needs. I'll get into the specifics of the equipment in the pages ahead, but the key is to cook "low and slow." That's the barbecue man's mantra and it's the most important thing you need to learn.

Cooking real barbecue takes a long time and a lot of patience. The right temperature for cooking barbecue is between 225° and 250°F. That's quite a bit lower than a typical cooking temperature in your indoor oven, so the food is naturally going to take longer to cook. A lot longer! For the beginning barbecue cook, it takes some time to accept that dinner needs to be started the day before you're planning to eat it, and that even then it may not be done exactly on time. There's an old saying among barbecue cooks that the food is "done when it's done." That may sound like a cliché, but it's not. To be a great barbecue cook you'll need to accept that. But if you start early and

explain that there will be a window for the time when dinner will be served, it'll work out. At first your friends will think you've gone a little crazy when they realize you've started dinner the night before and you still tell them to have another beverage because the food isn't ready yet. But after they taste the fruits of your labor, they will begin to understand and soon they'll be bringing you gifts of wood and spice and offering to help you tend the barbecue pit overnight.

You might be wondering why the meat needs to be cooked so slowly and so long. A lot of it has to do with the cuts of meat that are typically used for barbecue. The most common are pork shoulder or butt, beef brisket, and pork ribs. These are big cuts of meat and they take a long time to cook because of their size and makeup. They are tough and fatty and, frankly, they are the less desirable parts of the animal. At least they were less desirable until the pitmasters learned how to cook them properly! Now these cuts are all very popular and, of course, the prices have gone up accordingly. But no matter, these are the cuts that fit the barbecue cooking method the best so we continue to use them. I once had an old-school barbecue man in Albuquerque, Mr. Powdrell, tell me that he liked to cook big briskets

because they allowed him to cook them a long time. In this age of speeding everything up he wanted to slow things down. But that was because he understood that in the barbecue world, longer cooking makes things taste better.

The other constant element in making authentic barbecue is the flavor of smoking wood. The smoker that you use will dictate how the wood is incorporated, so read the instruction manual before you start. In most cases, the best way for a new barbecue cook to use wood is just to add some for flavor while using another source of fuel for heat. When you try to use wood for fuel you can easily use too much and oversmoke the food and that will ruin the meal. Charcoal is a great fuel for the home cook, but gas and electric will get the job done as well. I'll address the different styles of smokers and how to use them a little later, but your owner's manual should be specific about the best way to use your cooker and incorporate the wood. I haven't mentioned seasonings or barbecue sauces here and that's on purpose. Those are fine elements and we will use them later. A slow fire combined with wood smoke and meat is where the art of barbecue begins.

TOOLS AND TECHNIQUES

THE COOKERS

In the lingo of a barbecue man, the names "barbecue pit," "smoker," and "cooker" all mean the same thing. They are all the generic names for the unit we use to cook the barbecue. I'll give you the background on where these three names came from here but I will use them interchangeably throughout the book.

We use the name "barbecue pit" in reference to the origin of barbecue cooked in a big pit dug in the ground. This is still done in many places and it works well. The problem is you have to dig a huge hole in the ground and burn a whole lot of wood and this just isn't practical for most of us. I prefer to leave this method to my island friends, but I still respectfully use the term "pit" for anything I happen to be cooking my barbecue on.

"Smoker" is a popular name for a barbecue-cooking machine too, but it can be a little misleading. Cooking barbecue is surely a close cousin to the cold-smoking process, but it's not the same and the proper equipment for each is a little different. Cold-smoking to cure hams, bacon, salmon,

etc. is done at very low temps, usually under 100°F, and isn't intended to actually cook the protein in a traditional sense. It's really meant as a way to flavor and preserve cured food. Barbecue, on the other hand, is always cooked above 200°F and is definitely intended to cook the food. So while we're using smoke as part of the barbecue-cooking process, the equipment needs to be much more than just a smoker.

The third term, "barbecue cooker" or just "cooker," is commonly used by competition cooks because they use so many diverse styles of equipment at the same time. "Cooker" also helps avoid any confusion that might be created by the other two names.

Call it what you want, the only real requirements of your equipment for cooking barbecue are the ability to keep the temperature low and the heat source indirect. The temp can be kept low a lot of ways and if you're using electric or gas it will be as simple as turning down the dial on the thermostat. If you're using charcoal, there are two simple ways: You can simply build a small fire and add a bit of fuel as needed, or you can light a big pile in one or two places and then control the growth of the fire by closing down the air

vents—thus limiting the oxygen supply. Both ways work well and the one you choose will probably be dictated by the cooker that you choose.

Employing an indirect heat source is important and will help tame the fire as well. This can be achieved as simply as using a steel deflector or a big pan of water directly above the fire, or you can position the fire to the side of the food and funnel the heat sideways into the cooking chamber. In some extreme instances you can simply keep the food a great distance above the fire. Once again, the best way will be dictated by the cooker that you choose. So read on, look around, and then pick the style and size of cooker that you like and get cooking. Here are some of the more common cookers that work well for the beginner home cook along with a little description of each.

Vertical Water Smokers

These are also known as "bullet smokers" because of their shape. The design has the heat source on the bottom, a big pan of water directly above it, and the meat above the water on racks. There are usually two or three levels of food above the water. These smokers are very efficient and the water serves as a great equalizer by deflecting and absorbing the direct heat. The water may help keep things moist as well. They're typically small and inexpensive, and they work pretty well. It's a bit of a challenge getting to the fire and to the meat on the lower levels, but it's doable.

The most popular of these is the Weber Smokey Mountain Cooker and it comes in two sizes. It's fueled by charcoal, with wood chunks added for flavor. This is a well-made cooker and a great place to start for the home cook. You load up the charcoal, light it, stack up the cooker parts, and control the temp by opening and closing the air vents. Napoleon Grills has a very similar product called the Apollo that works even better. The Apollo as some innovations that make it a lot

more convenient to get to the lower-level food and the fire and it can be reduced in size for travel or small cooks. It all clips together for moving, which is a very nice upgrade. There are starter versions of this type of cooker that burn charcoal as well, but they aren't as refined and can be frustrating to cook on.

You'll also find propane gas versions of the vertical smoker, with a wood tray to hold chunks directly above the burner and the water pan directly above the wood. The big difference is that the gas models have a valve and thermostat. Set it and forget it. As with many things, the upgraded models work better than the entry level, but in general they all work pretty well. And while I prefer the taste of charcoal, the convenience of propane is something to be considered.

Electric Smokers

These may be the simplest of all to use. You'll need to keep some flavoring wood chunks around but these smokers don't use much of them and for fuel all you do is plug it into the wall. The electric element offers even heat and there's no chance of an off taste from it, so the concept is sound. You may find that electric smokers don't give a great color or "smoke ring" to the meat, but the taste will be as good as any other fuel you may choose. They are typically set up in a vertical arrangement with the heating element at the bottom, a tray to hold wood directly above that, a heat deflector or a pan of water, and finally racks to hold the meat. There are starter models that do pretty well, but they lack the mass of heavy steel and insulation to hold the heat in. The best one I've found is the Cookshack Smokette. It performs very well and is pretty much indestructible. This is a great choice for the condo balcony, where a live flame isn't allowed.

Gas Smokers

The gas smokers that you'll find for home use are similar to the electric units I've described previously. They have a gas

burner at the bottom, a tray to hold wood directly above that, a heat deflector or a pan of water, and, finally, racks to hold the meat. The big difference is that you'll need to keep a full propane bottle (or two) around for fuel. Most of the newer big barbecue restaurants use massive gas-assisted smokers, which means gas for heat and wood for flavor. These seem to work well for them and even though the home units are quite different, they work well, too. There are also a lot of gas grills that have a smoking tray built in. These will work pretty well to get you started, but if you cook a lot I think you'll find it best to have a dedicated smoker.

Ceramic Smokers

These have become very popular as a backyard smoker that also serves as your everyday grill and they really per-form well at both tasks. They look good, too! The whole grill is made out of heavy-duty ceramics, and once it heats up it will stay hot for many hours on very little fuel. Much like the vertical water smok-ers, you load the bottom with charcoal (lump charcoal only for these), and add wood chunks and chips for flavor. Light it, add the optional plate setter to act as a barrier, and then control the temp by

opening and closing the vents. You won't need a water pan when cooking with a ceramic smoker because of the ceramic plate setter, which acts as the barrier. The whole ceramic mass and small fire create evenly cooked food that always comes out moist and juicy. The leader in the industry is the Big Green Egg and they make five sizes. Many top chefs use these at home and it's no secret that I'm a big fan.

Pellet Smokers

Pellet smokers make the barbecue man's life very easy. You fill the hopper with wood pellets—a specially made item that looks like rabbit food but is made of sawdust—and set the thermostat and the food cooks. It's about that simple and they work well. Inside you'll find a

mechanical system that feeds the pellets to a burn pot underneath a deflector plate and as long as the electricity keeps working and the hopper stays full of dry pellets, you can smoke-cook real barbecue while you're sleeping. My only criticism of these is that they only do one thing—cook barbecue. Most of the other choices can cook a steak in a pinch but these really can't, unless you like a smoky, gray steak. The high-end version of these by Fast Eddy has become very popular on the competition circuit, and the backyard models by Traeger are doing well, too. You'll need to keep a supply of pellets on hand because they're only avail-able at specialty stores, and you won't be able to do much more than smoke on it, but these cook good barbecue and are a good choice for the home smoker.

Stovetop Smokers

Stovetop smokers are a nice alternative for the cook who just can't do it outside. There are two popular styles: The most common is made by Cameron and it looks like a cake pan with a sliding lid. But don't be fooled; it's actually a heavy-duty stainless-steel unit. The second one, and my favorite, is made by Nordic Ware and it looks like a Dutch oven with a domed lid similar to a backyard kettle grill. It even has the cute little spinner vent. Predictably, they call it the Indoor Stovetop Kettle Smoker.

Both styles work the same way. You put some fine-ground wood chips on the bottom, and a drip pan over that. A cooking grate goes next for the food to sit on. The lid then slides on for the Cameron or is placed on for the Nordic Ware and both provide a pretty good seal for indoor cooking. You'll want to keep your overhead vent fan running and your house will smell a bit of wood smoke, but I didn't find it to be much of a problem. Be sure to read the manufacturer's instructions to use these properly, but here are my tips: Don't overload the food. Every spot where the food is touching another piece won't be exposed to the smoke and won't pick up the flavor. This also applies to

covering up the cooking grate. The smoke needs to move around the chamber to get at the food and that's why I prefer the domed lid of the Nordic Ware model. There's just a little more room on top for bigger cuts of meat and the flow of the smoke. These indoor cookers work great on their own for quick-cook items like fish and shrimp. For longer-cooked items, I like to smoke them first on the stovetop and then finish in the oven or under the broiler for that great grilled color.

Offset Barbecue Pits

This is the classic black steel cooker with a side firebox where the fire is and a cooking chamber next to it where the food is. The smoke and fire pass through and over the meat on the way out the big exhaust stack on the other end. The origin of these pits is from the oilfields of Texas, where they were made using leftover pipe. This is by far the most macho-looking choice for any barbecue man and the big, heavy trailer models that you see the competition pros and caterers use do a great job. Unfortunately the home versions don't work nearly as well.

The concept is you have a big firebox and you start a wood fire in it. With the intake and exhaust vents wide open, the fire burns cleanly and heats the thick steel of the oil pipe as it slowly cooks the meat with only indirect heat entering the cooking chamber. But all that steel is very

heavy, so the home versions have to be lightened up for shipping and that's where the problems start. The fireboxes are made smaller and the whole pit is made of much thinner steel, so to keep the heat in, the vents need to be dampered down and then the fire doesn't burn as cleanly and the food gets too smoky. A simple solution is to use charcoal with wood added for flavor but that kind of defeats the whole purpose of having an offset cooker. The offset design is highly inefficient, which is fine when you're burning wood that you cut yourself, but not so good when you're buying charcoal. If you just can't resist the macho look of these, you'll still be able to cook good barbecue at home, you'll just use a lot of fuel and you'll need to work a little harder. The simple way to shop for these is to buy the heaviest one you can get.

Backyard Grills

You can smoke on just about any grill. Many will have a method for cooking indirectly and adding a little smoke, but if yours doesn't, you'll just need to get a little creative. For most charcoal grills you can push the coals to one side and place a drip pan under the meat. Add

some water or juice to the pan and you should be able to get pretty even indirect heat when the lid is closed. Keep the number of coals down and restrict the airflow a bit and you should be able to keep the temp down, too. If your grill is big enough and shaped properly, you can try putting a bank of coals on each side with the food in the middle. For smoke, adding wood chips that have been soaked in water is the best method for this type of setup. Adding wet chips also helps keep the fire low.

Your gas grill can do the job, too. Most have multiple burners and you'll need to turn some of them off and put the meat over the unlit ones. The burners on the other side will cook the meat slowly and indirectly. For example, if your grill has three burners side by side, turn the middle one off and put the meat there. You'll need to experiment to figure out which burners should be lit and how much flame from each is needed to get the temp right, but a little practice will get you there. You'll need to add wood, too. Many gas grills have a built-in smoker tray, but if yours doesn't you can buy an all-purpose smoker box at any grill or hardware store. There are many different backyard grills out there, so I'm not able to be too specific, but you can cook barbecue on them all with a little perseverance.

CHARCOAL AND WOOD

For the home barbecue cook, the idea of cooking with all wood may seem appealing but it's probably not going to work out. Most people prefer a mild smoke flavor and that's hard to achieve with a backyard smoker using all wood. So my advice is to use wood in the form of chips and chunks to add a smoky flavor to your fuel, which should be gas, electric, or charcoal. Of course this will be dictated by the cooker you have, but my preferred fuel is always charcoal.

There are two types of charcoal readily available, the briquettes that most Americans use and lump charcoal that the rest of the world uses. While briquettes do a very good job in most smokers, they are a fabricated product using charred wood and some other things to hold them together. Lump charcoal on the other hand is simply charred wood with nothing else added, so it's always my preference. It's also easier to light and it creates much less ash, a good thing when it's cleanup time. You may not be familiar with lump charcoal, but it's readily available. Look and ask around at the hardware store and the grocery store and you'll quickly find some. One thing to note—the density of lump charcoal is considerably less than briquettes, so you're going to need a bigger pile to get the same amount of cooking done. You'll quickly notice that a 20-pound bag of lump is about twice the size of a 20-pound bag of briquettes, so load your cooker accordingly.

The charcoal will give the food a little taste of smoke, but for real barbecue you'll want to add some wood for that true smoke flavor. The best choices for backyard cookers are chips and chunks. Chunks that are bagged for retail are typically about half the size of your fist and the chips you'll find are about the size of a quarter. Obviously, the chunks will provide heavier smoke than the chips, but that's not always what you want. More smoke isn't always better. Most people enjoy a light smoke flavor on their barbecue, so for a short smoke or small pieces of meat, chips may be the better choice. I prefer a combination of the two. This allows me to use a light amount of a strong wood combined with a heavier amount from a milder wood. For example, I'd use two chunks of cherry wood and two handfuls of hickory chips. So the next question is about the strong woods and the milder woods. Following are the most common cooking woods and the foods on which they work best. In the recipes, you'll find that I often like to use these woods in combination.

Alder

A mild smoke flavor. Use with salmon and other fish.

Apple

A light, sweet smoke flavor. Use alone with chicken, turkey, fish, ribs, pork, and beef. For ribs, pork, and beef, I like it best paired with a stronger wood like oak or hickory.

Cherry

A light, sweet smoke flavor. It seems to add a nice red hue to the meat. Use alone with chicken, turkey, fish, ribs, pork, and beef. For ribs, pork, and beef, I like it best paired with a stronger wood like oak or hickory.

Hickory

A strong smoke flavor but classic barbecue taste. Use very sparingly on chicken and turkey. Use alone or paired with a milder wood like apple or cherry for ribs, pork, or beef.

Mesquite

A very strong, distinctive taste. Use very sparingly for pork and beef. Best saved for occasional steak grilling.

Oak

A semi-strong smoke flavor but classic barbecue taste. Use sparingly on chicken and turkey. Use alone or paired with a milder wood like apple or cherry for ribs, pork, or beef.

Pecan

A middle-of-the-road taste and strength. Pecan seems to go well with everything when used in moderation.

You may also find some interesting exotic woods like the wine-soaked oak barrel pieces I've been getting from California or the very popular oak that comes from retired whiskey barrels. These are all fun to try as well. Don't get in a rut using the same wood all the time. As long as you don't use too much, I think that you'll find them mostly interchangeable.

As for the amounts of each wood, well that's going to be something you have to decide yourself. In the recipes I'll suggest light, medium, or heavy smoke, depending on the dish and the cooking time, but you'll have to figure out for yourself how much wood you'll need to achieve each designation. Every cooker is different and everybody's taste is different. I'd always suggest starting out with less and adding a little more each time to get it right where you want it. Food that's light in smoke flavor will still be enjoyed by everyone, but oversmoked food has an acrid, bitter taste that nobody will enjoy. Keep in mind that the cook who's been in the smoke all day may be less sensitive to the smoke flavor when it's dinner time. Many times the cook will find that the food tastes much smokier the next day to them because of this. Keep in mind that if your friends and family are saying the food is too smoky, it probably is.

BARBECUE TOOLS

Once you've got your cooker, fuel, and wood, it's time to get all your other tools in order for barbecue cooking. There really isn't a need for any gimmicky tools, barbecue cooking is pretty basic and straightforward. Prep the meat, place it in the smoker, and wait it out. You may already have a lot of the tools you need in the kitchen. Here are the tools I like to have around and a little description of how and why.

Aluminum Foil Pans

Aluminum foil pans are a barbecue man's best friend. The large ones work well when seasoning big cuts of meat. They contain the whole messy process and can be reused quite a few times. You can even use them on the grill and then toss them when the time comes. The old ones work well for ash and grease disposal, too. I keep large and medium pans around all the time and I find a good deal on them at a warehouse club.

Ash Tool

You'll need to stir the hot coals at some point before, during, or after the cooking, so make sure you have some sort of a tool for this. A fireplace poker, small shovel, or garden tool all work well.

BBQ Guru

The BBQ Guru is a temperature-control device that retrofits to any charcoal or wood cooker. It's really a pretty amazing little device that has a controller and a little fan that blows air on your fire as needed to keep the cooking temperature at your desired level. It makes just about any cooker automated so you can leave it unattended for hours while you sleep, shop, or work. My suggestion is to learn how to control your cooker on your own first, but once you know how to do it this device is a really great assistant.

Cooking Planks

Wooden cooking planks are a great way to create an indirect cooking setup on any grill, but they also add nice wood flavor and a flashy presentation at the table. The wood of choice is usually alder, but you'll also find cedar readily available, and even more exotic choices if you do a little searching. They're most commonly used for cooking salmon, and great for all kinds of seafood, but also for vegetables and even pork and beef. Just be sure to soak the plank in water for an hour before using.

Cutting Boards

I like lightweight polypropylene cutting boards for ease of cleanup, but wood and bamboo work just as well. I keep a couple small ones around for small projects and a big one for carving. There are also disposable cutting boards available that work very well for barbecue. Make a mess and throw it away. Look for those online.

Fire Extinguisher

It's always a good idea to have a fire extinguisher on hand when you're cooking with fire! Make sure it's an all-purpose model and that it's fully charged. This might be a good time to check that one in the kitchen, too.

Firestarters

Of course these are only for the charcoal users. If you're using briquettes, I'd strongly recommend a charcoal chimney. It looks kind of like a giant steel beer mug and it works really well. You load it with briquettes and crumple a couple sheets of newspaper in the bottom. Light it and come back in ten minutes to a flaming mug of charcoal. Just dump it into the firebox and you're ready to go. For most smokers you'll need to have a bed of additional charcoal, but it will quickly be lit by the hot coals from your chimney. You can use a chimney with lump charcoal as well, but it's not the best way. The lump lights so easily that you can just slip a couple paraffin/sawdust firestarter cubes into the pile, light them, and in ten minutes your pile will be burning in place. These paraffin starters are available in many shapes and should be easy to find at the grocery or hardware store. Please avoid using lighter fluid if you can. The flavor from the fluid carries over to the food and it's not pleasant.

Grill Brush

You'll need a long-handled grill brush to clean the cooking grid. These are readily available in all shapes and sizes. My favorite is a tool called the Billy Bar. It's more of a scraper than a brush, but it does a great job and it doubles as an ash tool (see page 21).

Grill Topper

These are perforated pans made for small items that will fall through the grates—like shrimp or cut vegetables—as well as big items that are hard to move around—like a pizza or a tender pork shoulder. They're often made of porcelain-coated steel and are easy to clean up. They come in many shapes and sizes. I like to have small and large sizes around and I use them often.

Heavy Gloves

You're going to have to handle something hot during the barbecue process, even if it's just the food, so you'll want to have some heavy-duty heatproof gloves. I like the big silicone mittens. I can grab anything with them and they clean up pretty well. Some cooks like big welding gloves, but I find they get pretty messy. Pick your favorites and keep them nearby, ready to go.

Knives

Barbecue doesn't require great knives, with the exception of the brisket slicer. And even for the brisket, a kitchen-grade knife like Forschner or Dexter-Russell will do fine. Just take care of them and keep them sharp and they will serve you well. For slicing that brisket, I like a 12-inch Granton-edge slicer and I rarely use it for anything else. When it's time to slice the brisket, nothing else will work and I want this one waiting and ready in tip-top shape. I also use a 7-inch boning knife a lot, mostly for trimming the meat before cooking, and a 10-inch chef's knife is always around in my kitchen. You may like different sizes; get what's comfortable and what you feel safe using. As with any other tool, you may want to upgrade to higher-quality knives. In general, German knives are a little heavier than their Japanese counterparts, so go to a store and try them out to see what fits your hand and budget the best. For my hand, the Shun Ken Onion knives are a great fit.

Latex Gloves

I like to have a box of latex gloves around, too. They're great for keeping your hands clean when you're cleaning up the cooker

or loading the charcoal. And of course they're great when you're handling the meat and rubbing it down. They come in different sizes and are available at warehouse clubs, restaurant supply stores, or the pharmacy. Some folks have an allergy to latex; they make nitrile and vinyl gloves that are very similar and solve that problem.

Meat Injectors

Sometimes it's best to inject the meat with a brine before cooking, so I like to keep a few of the cheap plastic food injectors around. There are fancy stainless-steel versions too, but they cost more and seem to have the same life expectancy as the plastic ones. If you're injecting a lot of meat at one time, look for a brine pump. It's a bigger commercial version and will last a long time.

Rib Rack

A rib rack is an important tool for the home barbecue cook. The main function of a rib rack is to make more room in the cooker, and since ribs take up a lot of grill space that's a good thing. There's no need to use it if there's room to lay the ribs flat, but if you need to stand them up it'll be a great help. Keep in mind that

ribs in a rack will need to be rotated and flipped so they'll cook evenly. Look for one that's tall and has wide slots. The bigger the better; just make sure it fits in your cooker.

Sheet Pans

I like to keep a few big sheet pans around for transferring the food in and out of the house. A jelly-roll pan is fine, but you might check out a warehouse club or restaurant supply store for some sheet pans that are a little more heavy duty.

Skewers

Big fancy metal skewers are great for kebobs, and lately I've been using a stainless-steel flexible skewer called the firewire, but I also use the little bamboo skewers a lot. Not only for serving as kebobs but also for cooking small things like shrimp and meatballs. It makes it easier to flip a bunch of them quickly, and you can remove the skewers before serving.

Smoker Box

A smoker box is a small metal box with holes in it that's made to hold wood chips. These are mostly used in gas grills

to get the wood chips down by the fire. Look for a lot of holes so the flames and heat can get in.

Spray Bottles and Mops

In old-school barbecue technique, the pitmasters used a mop sauce, which was a basting liquid typically made from beer, broth, vinegar, and aromatics to keep the meat moist during cooking. They'd apply this with a cotton mop, made in a small version for cooking, or with a big paintbrush. But most of the modern cookers keep the lid sealed pretty tight, creating a moist cooking environment. In most cases it's better to leave the lid closed than to open it and baste the food. But it's hard to teach an old hog new tricks, so sometimes I'll fill a spray bottle with apple juice spiked with a little whiskey to spritz the food when the lid is open.

Storage Bins

If you're storing your charcoal outside, a big plastic garbage can with a tight lid works well for storage. For wood chunks try plastic shoe boxes with the type of the wood written on them in marker.

Thermometers

The thermometer is one of the essential tools for cooking good barbecue. You'll need a couple different types for different uses. First you'll need one for checking the temperature in the cooker. This is often a stem thermometer that goes through the wall of the cooker. These are stationary and usually placed well above the food, where it's often 25 to 50 degrees hotter. Many cookers come with these already installed. If not you can use a remote instant-read thermometer, which has a readout base that stays outside with a cable and probe that go inside the cooker. These are nice because you can check the temperature near the grate, which is where the meat is cooking.

The other important thermometer is for checking the temperature of the food. The remote thermometer described above works well for this, too, and they even have units with dual probes to check the cooker temperature and the meat at the same time. Some models even take it a step further with a wireless readout unit that you can take in the house with you. Or you can go the simple route and get a handheld instant-read thermometer. I like these because you can check the meat in different places or check multiple pieces of meat very quickly. The absolute best in this category is the Superfast Thermapen by Thermoworks. Highly recommended.

Tongs, Spatulas, and Pig Tail Food Flippers

Big tongs to move big pieces of meat are going to be necessary. I always have a few pairs around—long and short. The long ones are nice to reach out over the fire, but sometimes you need the leverage of a couple pairs of short tongs to grab a heavy piece of meat. When cooking fish, you might want a big spatula. Then there's an interesting hook tool called the Pig Tail Food Flipper that can move some pretty big hunks of meat, but you could do it all with just tongs if you need to.

Vertical Chicken Stand

There are many versions of this handy tool. The one that holds a beer can works well and when you're done, you just toss the can. And there are some very complicated models that have a reservoir for liquid and a drip tray and even a top plug. I'm sure these work fine, but my favorite is the plain wire Christmas tree–looking stand. I use that in a disposable round cake pan and I feel like the liquid flavors the whole chicken instead of just the inside.

Wide Heavy-Duty Aluminum Foil

You're going to be handling large cuts of meat and you're going to need to wrap it and cover it, both hot off the grill and when storing in the refrigerator. Be sure to have a good supply of wide heavy-duty aluminum foil around at all times.

Zip-top Plastic Bags

I always keep the gallon size around for marinating and storing leftovers. A hint is to buy the freezer bags, because they're heavier duty and less likely to leak.

SPICES AND SAUCES

Barbecue sauce does not make meat *barbecue*. Adding barbecue sauce to meat that's baked or cooked in a slow cooker may make a tasty dinner, but it isn't real barbecue. Once you master the technique of slow-smoked barbecue, you'll find that you and your guests will understand this and begin to enjoy the meat itself, and barbecue sauce consumption at your house will go way down. The twang of a vinegar sauce and the sweet-spicy taste of a tomato-based barbecue sauce are nice complements to the smoky meat, but they don't define it. Barbecue sauce is a condiment. In most of the recipes here you'll find the sauce either served on the side or brushed on very late as a finishing glaze. So if it's not about the sauce, then what does define real barbecue?

Barbecue is simply the meat, slow-cooked with wood smoke for flavor. But the meat does need a little seasoning to help bring out the flavor. Salt and pepper will suffice and are still the tradition in some of the old barbecue joints, but for most of us a more complex barbecue rub has become the norm. These can range from simple to elaborate. On the simple end is a combination of salt, pepper, garlic powder, and a little paprika. The more complex versions will typically add sugar, and then any and all of the other things in the spice cabinet. From predictable flavorings like chili powder, cumin, and thyme to more adventurous items like dried orange peel, coriander, and chipotle powder, it can all work in a barbecue rub. The trick is using ingredients that complement each other and getting the ratio just right. Like any other cooking, it's all about balance.

> The trick is using ingredients that complement each other and getting the ratio just right. Like any other cooking, it's all about balance.

The rub recipes in this book are all good, but don't be afraid to tweak them to your liking, or just make up your own from scratch, using mine as a guideline. Make a small batch and measure everything as it goes in, so you can re-create it later. Taste your new rub by itself, but also be sure to try it on cooked food. Since many of the barbecue recipes take a long time to cook, you'll need a little quicker test. I like to cut a pork chop into small pieces for testing. Season a small piece with your rub and cook it in a sauté pan to see what you think. If it needs a little tweaking, do that and then season another small piece, etc., until you get it where you want it. The taste will change when it slow-cooks on the barbecue pit but if it tastes good on a sautéed pork chop, it's a pretty good start.

It's always smart to buy good-quality fresh ingredients to make your rubs. The supermarket can be okay, and I rarely suggest any ingredients that aren't available there, but there are a lot of local spice purveyors around these days and their stuff is usually fresher and cheaper. I buy a lot of spices online, too. My favorite source is Pendery's in Fort Worth, Texas. Their ground chiles and chile blends are a cut above most and well above the stuff at the supermarket.

Don't be a barbecue snob who thinks sauce is evil. Just serve it on the side and let your guests decide how they like it.

The rules are the same for barbecue sauces, glazes, and marinades. If you start with good-quality ingredients, you will get good results. And while the sauce really doesn't define real barbecue, people sure do like it. So while I may prefer mine "dry," meaning without sauce, I always have barbecue sauce available for my guests—and sometimes more than one. I serve a traditional red, sweet barbecue sauce, but I also like to add an exotic option like a vinegar sauce. There are some good barbecue sauce recipes here, and while I make fresh sauces at home, there are many great commercial barbecue sauces available these days, too. Many big food companies have expanded their lines to cover the different tastes and regions of barbecue and some of these are very good products. There are also literally hundreds of small-batch barbecue sauces being made around the country and many of them are unique and very good. Don't be a barbecue snob who thinks sauce is evil. Just serve it on the side and let your guests decide how they like it. I like to put the shaker of rub on the table for them as well. The recipes that are in this chapter have all been created for recipes later in the book, but please feel free to mix and match them as you please. You'll be a much better pitmaster when you learn to adapt any recipe to the taste that you and your guests prefer.

BARBECUE RUB #67

MAKES ABOUT
1½
CUPS

After a lot of years of making barbecue rubs, I've used up all the good names, so sometimes I just use numbers now. Numbers 67 and 68 are a little tip of the hat to the band named after my hometown, Chicago. This one is a great all-around rub for the new barbecue cook because it's good on just about everything.

Combine all the ingredients in a medium bowl and mix well. The rub may be stored in an airtight container in a cool place for up to 6 months.

½ cup Sugar in the Raw

½ cup kosher salt

3 tablespoons chili powder

3 tablespoons paprika

1 teaspoon garlic powder

1 teaspoon onion powder

½ teaspoon black pepper

½ teaspoon lemon pepper

½ teaspoon ground coffee

¼ teaspoon cayenne pepper

BARBECUE RUB #68

MAKES ABOUT
1½
CUPS

½ cup packed light brown
sugar, dried (see Note)

⅓ cup kosher salt

¼ cup paprika

1 tablespoon chili powder

2 teaspoons garlic powder

1 teaspoon Sugar in the Raw

1 teaspoon onion powder

1 teaspoon black pepper

1 teaspoon dried basil

½ teaspoon ground cumin

½ teaspoon turmeric

¼ teaspoon cayenne pepper

This rub is a little more complex than Barbecue Rub #67 (page 29) and has great color as it cooks on the food. I like to put this one in the food processor until it's finely ground. It makes for a smooth texture but also takes care of breaking up the lumps in the dried brown sugar. You may want to dry the sugar the day before. This preparation is a little more complicated, but don't be afraid to use on whatever you're cooking.

Combine all the ingredients in the bowl of a food processor fitted with a metal blade. Process for 15 seconds. The rub may be stored in an airtight container in a cool place for up to 6 months.

Note: To dry the brown sugar, spread it out on a sheet pan and let it sit overnight, or preheat your oven to 200°F, then shut it off and put the sheet in for 10 minutes.

RAY'S SUPERSWEET RIB RUB

This rub is extra-sweet and goes really well with ribs and other cuts of pork. It is a good choice if you like to serve your ribs dry. The sweetness will have guests thinking you used barbecue sauce. This one isn't recommended for hot grilling because all that sugar makes it burn pretty easily. I like to mix it in the food processor for a finer grind, but if you like it coarse just mix it in a bowl.

Combine all the ingredients in the bowl of a food processor with a metal blade. Process for 5 seconds, until the lumps are gone. The rub may be stored in an airtight container in a cool place for up to 6 months.

½ cup Sugar in the Raw

½ cup packed light brown sugar

½ cup kosher salt

3 tablespoons chili powder

1 tablespoon ground cumin

2 teaspoons black pepper

2 teaspoons onion powder

1 teaspoon garlic powder

1 teaspoon dried grated orange peel

¼ teaspoon ground thyme

¼ teaspoon cinnamon

¼ teaspoon ground chipotle (or cayenne pepper)

MAKES ABOUT

1

CUP

CHICAGO RAY'S PRIME RIB RUB

½ cup kosher salt

¼ cup coarsely ground black pepper

2 tablespoons granulated garlic

1 teaspoon Sugar in the Raw

1 teaspoon chili powder

1 teaspoon paprika

1 teaspoon dried thyme

1 teaspoon dried marjoram

This rub is outstanding on grilled steaks and smoked prime rib. It's really just a seasoned salt and it works well for everyday use around the kitchen, so don't save it for the big beef. For you carb counters, simply skip the sugar. The rub will still be quite good and carb free.

Combine all the ingredients in a medium bowl and mix well. The rub may be stored in an airtight container in a cool place for up to 6 months.

MAKES ABOUT

1

CUP

¼ cup kosher salt

¼ cup chili powder

1 teaspoon ground chipotle

1 teaspoon ground cumin

1 teaspoon onion powder

½ teaspoon garlic powder

½ teaspoon black pepper

½ teaspoon lemon pepper

¼ teaspoon cayenne pepper

DR. BBQ'S FIRED-UP FAJITA RUB

This is a big, bold, spicy rub that will really fire things up! This one's not for the meek and mild eaters! It's great for fajita or taco meat, where the tortillas will help mellow things out. But also try it on meats that will be used as part of a salad. It just might help out your pot of chili, too.

Combine all the ingredients in a medium bowl and mix well. The rub may be stored in an airtight container in a cool place for up to 6 months.

SUPERCHICKEN WING RUB

Chicken wings are really tasty and versatile, so they're a lot of fun for the cook. You can mix and match a lot of different ingredients when seasoning them. This rub uses the great flavor of citrus combined with a little heat to really brighten up the taste. If you like your wings hot, just add a little more cayenne to the mix.

Combine all the ingredients in the bowl of a food processor fitted with a metal blade. Process for 5 seconds, until the lumps are gone. The rub may be stored in an airtight container in a cool place for up to 6 months.

½ cup kosher salt

½ cup Sugar in the Raw

1 tablespoon sugar

1 tablespoon paprika

1 teaspoon onion powder

1 teaspoon garlic powder

1 teaspoon dried grated orange peel

1 teaspoon lemon pepper

½ teaspoon black pepper

½ teaspoon ground thyme

½ teaspoon cayenne pepper

¼ teaspoon turmeric

HERBY RUB

MAKES ABOUT
3/4
CUP

¼ cup kosher salt

¼ cup Sugar in the Raw

1 teaspoon granulated garlic

1 teaspoon granulated onion

1 teaspoon dry mustard powder

1 teaspoon dried oregano

1 teaspoon dried tarragon

1 teaspoon dried thyme

1 teaspoon dried basil

1 teaspoon lemon pepper

1 teaspoon black pepper

¼ teaspoon turmeric

I find that dried herbs work best for a barbecue rub, so that's what I've used here. But if the garden is flourishing and you want to try it with fresh herbs, by all means go for it. You may want to add a little olive oil to hold it all together. I like this on lamb, fish, pork, and vegetables.

Combine all the ingredients in the bowl of a food processor fitted with a metal blade. Process for 2 seconds. The rub may be stored in an airtight container in a cool place for up to 6 months.

REAL NORTH CAROLINA VINEGAR SAUCE

MAKES ABOUT

1 ¾

CUPS

The true barbecue sauces of North Carolina are very simple and very tangy. Some might even be considered hard-core because of the amount of straight vinegar they use. Many times they are just vinegar with a little sugar and red pepper flakes. This sauce represents the western North Carolina style and the type that would appeal to more people outside of the region. It's really good on smoked pork and that's just about all they serve in North Carolina.

In a medium saucepan over medium heat, combine the vinegar, ketchup, brown sugar, salt, Worcestershire, and red pepper flakes. Bring to a simmer, stirring often, and cook for 3 minutes, until well blended. Remove from the heat and serve, or cool and store the sauce in an airtight container in the refrigerator for up to I week.

1 cup cider vinegar

⅔ cup ketchup

1 tablespoon brown sugar

1 teaspoon kosher salt

1 teaspoon Worcestershire sauce

½ teaspoon red pepper flakes

¼ cup butter

1 small yellow onion, finely chopped

3 garlic cloves, crushed

1 jalapeño, seeded and minced (leave the seeds in if you like it hot)

½ teaspoon celery seed

2 cups ketchup

½ cup cider vinegar

½ cup honey

⅓ cup yellow mustard

¼ cup apple juice

2 tablespoons soy sauce

2 tablespoons Worcestershire sauce

1 tablespoon Louisiana hot sauce

1 tablespoon tomato paste

1 teaspoon liquid smoke (optional)

½ teaspoon salt

½ teaspoon black pepper

THICK AND RICH BARBECUE SAUCE

MAKES ABOUT
1
QUART

This is a big, thick, red barbecue sauce made with fresh ingredients and a lot of love in your kitchen. Every barbecue cook I have ever known has a mother sauce they've been working on for years, and this would be a great place to start on yours. You can skip the liquid smoke if you like, but I think it adds a nice layer.

In a medium saucepan over medium heat, melt the butter. Add the onion, garlic, and jalapeño and cook for about 8 minutes, stirring occasionally, until soft. Add the celery seed and mix well. Cook for 1 minute. Add the ketchup, vinegar, honey, mustard, apple juice, soy sauce, Worcestershire, hot sauce, tomato paste, liquid smoke (if using), salt, and pepper. Mix well and bring to a simmer. Cook for 20 minutes, mixing often, until thickened. Remove from the heat and serve, or cool and store the sauce in an airtight container in the refrigerator for up to 1 week.

THIN AND SPICY BARBECUE SAUCE

MAKES 2½ CUPS

Some people don't like a big, thick, rich barbecue sauce because they feel it masks the true flavor of the meat. This sauce is thin, and a light coating will complement any barbecued meat nicely without taking over. You can skip the cayenne to tone it down a little or use the spicy V8 to crank it up a lot.

In a medium saucepan over medium heat, combine the tomato juice, V8, honey, vinegar, soy sauce, Worcestershire, sugar, steak sauce, pepper, chili powder, onion powder, garlic powder, celery seed, chipotle, and cayenne. Bring to a simmer, stirring often, and cook for 3 minutes, until well blended. Remove from the heat and serve, or cool and store the sauce in an airtight container in the refrigerator for up to 1 week.

1 cup tomato juice

½ cup V8 juice

½ cup honey

¼ cup cider vinegar

2 tablespoons soy sauce

1 tablespoon Worcestershire sauce

1 tablespoon Sugar in the Raw

1 tablespoon A.1. Steak Sauce

1 teaspoon black pepper

1 teaspoon chili powder

1 teaspoon onion powder

1 teaspoon garlic powder

¼ teaspoon celery seed

¼ teaspoon ground chipotle

¼ teaspoon cayenne pepper

1½ cups yellow mustard

1 cup cider vinegar

1 cup packed brown sugar

¼ cup ketchup

¼ cup honey

2 teaspoons
Worcestershire sauce

1 teaspoon onion powder

1 teaspoon garlic powder

1 teaspoon kosher salt

1 teaspoon black pepper

2 teaspoons Louisiana
hot sauce (optional)

YELLOW BARBECUE SAUCE

This is a great version of a yellow mustard barbecue sauce. It's not your typical sweet barbecue sauce, with the twang of the mustard as a base. This type of sauce has been popular in the barbecue regions of South Carolina and parts of Georgia for a long time, but lately it's really starting to catch on all around the country with mustard and barbecue lovers.

In a medium saucepan over medium heat, combine the mustard, vinegar, brown sugar, ketchup, honey, Worcestershire, onion powder, garlic powder, salt, and pepper. Bring to a simmer, stirring often, and cook for 3 minutes, until well blended. Remove from the heat and mix in the hot sauce (if using). Serve, or cool and store the sauce in an airtight container in the refrigerator for up to 1 week.

ORANGE-CHIPOTLE BARBECUE SAUCE

MAKES ABOUT
2
CUPS

Those little smoked jalapeños we know as chipotles have a ton of big flavor and quite a spicy kick! They match beautifully with the sweet citrus flavor of the orange juice in this sauce. The balance of these two big tastes matches up nicely with any grilled pork dish, but especially ribs. This one may become your new favorite barbecue sauce.

In a small saucepan over medium heat, combine the orange juice and tomato sauce. Bring to a simmer and cook for about 15 minutes, until reduced by one third. Add the honey, chipotle puree, salt, pepper, cumin, onion powder, and garlic powder. Mix well. Return to a simmer and cook for 10 minutes, until the flavors have combined and the sauce has thickened. Add a little more orange juice if it gets too thick. Remove from the heat and serve, or cool and store the sauce in an airtight container in the refrigerator for up to 1 week.

Note: To make chipotle puree, put a can of chipotles in adobo sauce in a blender and blend on medium speed for 1 to 2 minutes, until fully pureed. Use in sauces and stews.

1½ cups orange juice, plus more if needed

1½ cups tomato sauce

2 tablespoons honey

1 tablespoon chipotle puree (see Note)

½ teaspoon salt

½ teaspoon black pepper

½ teaspoon ground cumin

½ teaspoon onion powder

½ teaspoon garlic powder

DR PEPPER BARBECUE SAUCE

MAKES ABOUT
2¼
CUPS

1 quart Dr Pepper

1 cup ketchup

2 tablespoons cider vinegar

2 tablespoons soy sauce

1 tablespoon Worcestershire sauce

1 teaspoon onion powder

1 teaspoon garlic powder

1 teaspoon black pepper

¼ teaspoon dried grated orange peel

The deep cherry flavor and sweet syrup consistency of Dr Pepper are a great place to start a barbecue sauce recipe. The finished sauce has just a hint of the soda pop when it pairs up with the meat. Hide the bottle and keep the secret to see if your guests can figure out what that familiar taste really is. This rich-tasting sauce goes well with smoked pork and beef.

In a medium saucepan over medium-high heat, bring the Dr Pepper to a fast simmer. Cook until the Dr Pepper is reduced to 1 cup, about 25 minutes. Add the ketchup, vinegar, soy sauce, Worcestershire, onion powder, garlic powder, pepper, and orange peel. Mix well and return to a simmer. Lower the heat and cook at a low simmer for 5 minutes, stirring often, until well blended and thickened. Remove from the heat and serve, or cool and store the sauce in an airtight container in the refrigerator for up to 1 week.

BANANA KETCHUP

Banana ketchup is a very popular condiment in the Philippines. It's really not like the processed tomato product that we're used to, but it's fun to make and a very new taste to most Americans. It's a little sweet and a little tangy and a lot of tasty. It goes well with smoked pork and chicken for something a little different.

In a medium saucepan over medium heat, heat the peanut oil. Add the onion, garlic, jalapeño, and ginger. Cook for about 6 minutes, stirring occasionally, until the onion is translucent. Add the turmeric and allspice, mix well, and cook for 1 minute. Add the bananas and mix well. Add the vinegar, honey, rum, tomato paste, soy sauce, and salt. Mix well and bring to a simmer. Cover and cook for 15 minutes, stirring often. Remove from the heat to cool. When cool, pour the sauce into a food processor fitted with a metal blade and process for about 1 minute, until smooth. Serve at room temperature. Store in an airtight container in the refrigerator for up to 2 weeks.

2 tablespoons peanut oil

1 small sweet onion, finely chopped

2 garlic cloves, crushed

1 jalapeño, seeded and minced (leave the seeds in if you like it hot)

1 tablespoon crushed peeled fresh ginger

½ teaspoon turmeric

½ teaspoon ground allspice

4 ripe bananas, mashed

½ cup white vinegar

2 tablespoons honey

2 tablespoons rum

1 tablespoon tomato paste

1 tablespoon soy sauce

½ teaspoon salt

RIBS RULE THE WORLD

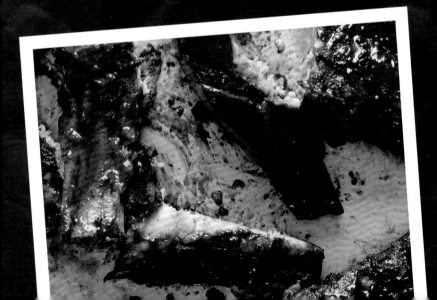

There is no more passionate subject in the world of barbecue than ribs. I've never met a barbecue fan who didn't have a rib story to tell. It might be about some ribs their uncle cooked or a slab they ate at a famous barbecue joint or their own personal secret sauce that is going to make them famous someday, but no matter who it is they have a story. While many of the geographical regions count their preferred barbecue meat to be beef brisket, pork shoulder, or even lamb, they all still like pork ribs. In Texas, beef is by far the most popular menu item in barbecue joints and for home cooks. When you go to the grocery store in Texas, you'll find the meat case chock-full of briskets. But right there next to them are the pork ribs. In the barbecue joints of Kansas City, brisket is by far the number-one item. Some of the old places have been slicing and serving it for over eighty years! But they also sell a lot of pork ribs. An interesting side note is that pulled pork has found its way into these bastions of beef in recent years—mainly because folks hear about it being served in other regions and they ask for it. I say give the folks in Texas and Kansas City a few more decades to get their pulled pork down. Have the pork ribs instead.

But when you travel to Tennessee, Georgia, North Carolina, and even Florida, you'll find people who have been cooking pulled pork for hundreds of years. Whole hogs and pork shoulders are simply called "barbecue" in these parts. It's what they know and love and if you see brisket on the menu you prob-ably shouldn't order it. Much like their beef brothers,

they've begun cooking other things because people are asking for it, but pork ribs have always been there and continue to be popular. Even in the great northern cities, where until recently they really didn't know much about barbecue, they have always eaten some version of barbecued pork ribs. They may not have known how to cook them properly, but they tried. By the way, that's where the evil tradition of boiling the ribs began. Rib boiling is a simple subject: Don't do it!

There is no more passionate subject in the world of barbecue than ribs. I've never met a barbecue fan who didn't have a rib story to tell.

There are a few different cuts of pork ribs and they have their individual fans as well. The cut we know as "baby back ribs" doesn't really come from a baby hog. These come from the top of the hog and are what I'd consider to be the white meat. It's a little leaner and more tender, and the slabs are a little smaller. The bones pull apart nicely for eating and they have that great name. All these things have made baby back ribs seem to be a little more uptown and they are popular up north. In the South, barbecue fans seem to like a little more of a rustic rib, so spareribs are the norm. These come from the side of the hog, and have a good fat content, kind of like the dark meat of a hog. They're a little bigger and more cumbersome to eat, with the cartilage of the rib tips still attached, but in the world of rib eating a little gnawing isn't really a bad thing. You'll need to cut through each rib individually to serve the spareribs properly, but for many of us the great taste is worth the trouble. The last cut is the St. Louis–style pork rib. These are simply spareribs with the tips cut off. The tips are the cartilage part of the spareribs and the thing that makes them a little more challenging to eat. Cutting the tips off makes a neat slab kind of like a baby back rib, but with that great taste of the dark meat. These are the favorite of most of the barbecue cook-off champions. The tips that are left over are a delicacy in their own right. They're probably the tastiest part of all ribs, but they lack in popularity because they are just kind of messy to eat.

The basic cooking process for these three types of ribs is pretty consistent. First thing you need to do is peel off the membrane from the bone side. Loosen it up with a dull tool like a butter knife, and then peel it off. Some days it comes off in one sheet and other days it's a few pieces, but after a few tries you'll get the hang of it. The next step is to smoke the ribs for that great barbecue flavor. Once they're all browned up and looking good, they get wrapped in aluminum foil, maybe with a little liquid, then back in the smoker until tender. Once they're tender, you can eat them or finish them back on the cooker with a sauce, glaze, or dry rub.

There is a fourth cut of pork rib and this one is a little confusing. Country-style ribs used to be the last few rib bones with the pork chop meat from the loin attached and butterflied. But butchering has changed and some of the cuts have too. These days you may find the old-style loin country-style pork ribs, but it's more likely that you'll find a shoulder cut with the same name. On top of that you will find the shoulder cut with and without the bone. These shoulder ribs aren't really ribs, but they are tasty so I've included a recipe for them here.

. . . for many of us, barbecue is all about the ribs.

Last, but not least, I need to mention beef ribs. Because of the size of the animal these are just not the same as pork ribs. They're much bigger and the meat is much tougher, but with the right care they can be delicious from the barbecue pit. I've included a couple recipes here, but for most of us the truth is barbecued ribs are all about the pork. And for many of us, barbecue is all about the ribs.

MEMPHIS-STYLE WET BABY BACK RIBS

MAKES
9
SERVINGS

The dry-rubbed ribs in Memphis get a lot of attention, but they're serving plenty of wet ribs there too. Most of the barbecue restaurants specialize in one style or the other, but even the hard-core dry-rub places will have some sauce around and it's always good. If you like your ribs a little sweeter and a little stickier, these are for you. This recipe would be a great place to begin your rib-cooking journey. They're the style of ribs that most people like and even if you don't get them perfect the first time, they'll be darn good.

Peel the membrane off the back of the ribs and trim any excess fat. In a small bowl, mix together the Barbecue Rub #67 and the Barbecue Rub #68. Sprinkle the mixture on the ribs using about two thirds on the meat side and one third on the bone side. Refrigerate for 30 minutes.

3 full slabs baby back ribs
(about 2 pounds each)

¼ cup Barbecue Rub #67
(page 29)

¼ cup Barbecue Rub #68
(page 30)

1 cup Thick and Rich Barbecue Sauce (page 38), plus extra for serving

continued

Prepare your cooker to cook indirectly at 235°F using a combination of one third hickory and two thirds cherry wood for smoke flavor. Put the ribs in the cooker, bone-side down. Cook the ribs for 2 hours, then flip and cook for 30 minutes longer, until the ribs are nicely browned.

Lay out three double-thick sheets of heavy-duty aluminum foil. Lay one slab on each piece of foil. Close up the rib packages, pressing out as much air as possible. Do not seal the packages tightly; they need to breathe a little.

Return to the cooker for I hour, or until tender. Check for doneness by pushing a toothpick into the meat. It should go in and out very easily. Transfer the ribs to a sheet pan. Remove from the foil and brush the meaty side with the barbecue sauce. Return to the cooker for I5 minutes. Cut each slab into three pieces, transfer to a platter, and serve with additional barbecue sauce on the side.

3 full slabs baby back ribs
(about 2 pounds each)

¼ cup Barbecue Rub #67
(page 29)

¼ cup Barbecue Rub #68
(page 30), plus 3 tablespoons

3 tablespoons apple juice

MEMPHIS-STYLE DRY BABY BACK RIBS

If you order ribs in a Memphis barbecue restaurant, you'll have to decide if you want them "wet" or "dry." Most places specialize in one or the other, but when pressed will serve you what you want. My favorite is always the dry ribs, but it's not as simple as leaving the sauce off. Dry rubs flavor dry ribs and are made to be served without sauce. They even add a little extra rub right before serving.

Peel the membrane off the back of the ribs and trim any excess fat. In a small bowl, mix together the Barbecue Rub #67 and the ¼ cup Barbecue Rub #68. Sprinkle the mixture on the ribs using about two thirds on the meat side and one third on the bone side. Refrigerate for 30 minutes.

Prepare your cooker to cook indirectly at 235°F using a combination of one third hickory and two thirds cherry wood for smoke flavor. Put the ribs in the cooker, bone-side down. Cook the ribs for 2 hours, then flip and cook for 30 minutes longer, until the ribs are nicely browned.

Lay out three double-thick sheets of heavy-duty aluminum foil. Lay one slab on each piece of foil. Close up the rib packages, pressing out as much air as possible. Do not seal the packages tightly; they need to breathe a little.

Return to the cooker for I hour, or until tender. Check for doneness by pushing a toothpick into the meat. It should go in and out very easily. Transfer the ribs to a sheet pan. Remove from the foil and brush the meaty side with the apple juice. Sprinkle I tablespoon of the Barbecue Rub #68 over the meaty side of each slab of ribs. Cut each slab into three pieces to serve.

ASIAN-SAUCED BABY BACK RIBS

3 full slabs baby back ribs (about 2 pounds each)

Barbecue Rub #67 (page 29)

ASIAN BARBECUE SAUCE

½ cup hoisin sauce

¼ cup soy sauce

¼ cup honey

¼ cup barbecue sauce

2 tablespoons white vinegar

1 tablespoon sesame oil

½ teaspoon sriracha hot sauce

These ribs get a typical barbecue rub and typical American barbecue cooking, but the sauce comes from a whole different culture. The Asian flavors match up beautifully with smoked pork and especially ribs. You can try serving these ribs alongside some with a traditional barbecue sauce and let guests compare the interesting differences in the flavor profiles.

Peel the membrane off the back of the ribs and trim any excess fat. Sprinkle the rub on the ribs using about two thirds on the meat side and one third on the bone side. Refrigerate for 30 minutes.

Prepare your cooker to cook indirectly at 235°F using cherry wood for smoke flavor. Put the ribs in the cooker bone-side down. Cook the ribs for 2 hours, then flip and cook for 30 minutes longer, until the ribs are nicely browned.

To make the sauce: Combine the hoisin sauce, soy sauce, honey, barbecue sauce, vinegar, sesame oil, and sriracha in a small saucepan, over medium heat. Bring to a simmer, stirring often until combined. Remove from the heat and set aside.

Lay out three double-thick sheets of heavy-duty aluminum foil. Lay one slab on each piece of foil. Close up the rib packages, pressing out as much air as possible. Do not seal the packages tightly; they need to breathe a little.

Return to the cooker for 1 hour, or until tender. Check for doneness by pushing a toothpick into the meat. It should go in and out very easily. Transfer the ribs to a sheet pan. Remove from the foil and brush the meaty side with some of the sauce. Return to the cooker for 15 minutes. Cut each slab into three pieces, transfer to a platter, and serve with additional sauce on the side.

2 slabs pork spareribs
(3½ to 4 pounds each)

Barbecue Rub #68
(page 30)

½ cup apple juice

Yellow Barbecue Sauce
(page 40)

SPARERIBS WITH YELLOW BARBECUE SAUCE

Mustard-based barbecue sauces are very popular in South Carolina and parts of Georgia, and when I think of those places I think of old-fashioned pork barbecue. And nothing goes better with yellow barbecue sauce than full-cut spareribs. The big pork flavor of these ribs and the tangy, sharp mustard flavor are a perfect match.

Prepare your cooker to cook indirectly at 235°F using medium hickory wood for smoke flavor.

Peel the membrane off the back of the ribs. Remove the flap of meat on the back and trim any excess fat. Season the ribs liberally with the rub on both sides. Put the ribs in the cooker, bone-side down, and cook for 2 hours. Flip the ribs and cook for 1 hour more.

Lay out two double-thick sheets of heavy-duty aluminum foil. Lay one slab on each piece of foil, meat-side up. Fold the foil up around the ribs and add ¼ cup of the apple juice to each packet. Complete the wrapping, closing up the rib packages, pressing out as much air as possible. Do not seal the packages tightly; they need to breathe a little.

Return to the cooker for I hour. Remove the ribs from the cooker. Open the packages, take the ribs out of the foil, and discard the foil and juices. Baste the ribs well on both sides with the barbecue sauce. Return to the cooker for 30 minutes, or until tender. Check for doneness by pushing a toothpick into the meat. It should go in and out very easily. When they're as you like them, transfer to a platter and tent loosely with foil. Let the ribs rest in the foil for at least 5 minutes. Discard the foil and juices. Slice each rib individually and transfer to a platter to serve.

2 slabs pork spareribs
(3½ to 4 pounds each)

Salt

Black pepper

Garlic powder

½ cup apple juice

ROADSIDE BARBECUE SPARERIBS

This recipe is for the most basic of all barbecued ribs—the kind you'll find served on the side of the road by a real barbecue man on weekends throughout the South. The ingredients are very simple and so is the cooking method, but if you like pork and wood smoke you're going to love these.

Prepare your cooker to cook indirectly at 235°F using medium hickory wood for smoke flavor.

Peel the membrane off the back of the ribs. Remove the flap of meat on the back and trim any excess fat. Season the ribs liberally with salt, pepper, and garlic powder on both sides. Put the ribs in the cooker, bone-side down, and cook for 2 hours. Flip the ribs and cook for 1 hour more.

Lay out two double-thick sheets of heavy-duty aluminum foil. Lay one slab on each piece of foil, meat-side up. Fold the foil up around the ribs and add ¼ cup of the apple juice to each packet. Complete the wrapping, closing up the rib packages, pressing out as much air as possible. Do not seal the packages tightly; they need to breathe a little.

Return to the cooker for 1 hour. Open the package and check for doneness by pushing a toothpick into the meat. It should go in and out very easily. If you want the ribs more tender, just wrap them back up and cook a little longer. When they're as you like them, remove from the heat. Let the ribs rest in the foil for at least 5 minutes. Discard the foil and juices. Slice each rib individually and transfer to a platter to serve.

ST. LOUIS–CUT RIBS WITH ORANGE-CHIPOTLE BARBECUE SAUCE

2 slabs St. Louis–cut pork ribs
(about 2½ pounds each)

Barbecue Rub #67 (page 29)

Orange-Chipotle Barbecue
Sauce (page 41)

The St. Louis cut of ribs is simply the whole spareribs with the bottom cartilage removed. They're a little easier to eat this way, but still have that great spare-rib taste. The Orange-Chipotle Barbecue Sauce really brightens up these ribs. Chipotles are smoked jala-peños, and they add a great smoky and spicy flavor. If you like the ribs spicier, just add some more of the chipotle paste to the sauce.

Prepare your cooker to cook indirectly at 235°F using medium apple wood for smoke flavor.

Peel the membrane off the back of the ribs and trim any excess fat. Season the ribs liberally on both sides with the rub. Place in the smoker, meat-side up, and cook for 2 hours. Flip the ribs and cook for 45 minutes.

Divide the sauce equally between two bowls. Reserve one for serving.

Lay out two double-thick sheets of heavy-duty aluminum foil. Lay one slab on each piece of foil, meat-side up. Brush the top of the ribs heavily with half of the barbecue sauce. Close up the rib packages, pressing out as much air as possible. Do not seal the packages tightly; they need to breathe a little.

Return to the cooker for 30 minutes. Open the package and check for doneness by pushing a toothpick into the meat. It should go in and out very easily. If you want the ribs more tender, just wrap them back up and cook a little longer. When they're as you like them, remove from the heat and let rest in the foil for at least 10 minutes. Slice each rib individually and transfer to a platter to serve.

BARBECUE CHAMPIONSHIP RIBS

MAKES
4 TO 6
SERVINGS

The ribs that are prepared for the big cook-offs from around the country are quite different from what you would normally cook at home or eat in a restaurant. Over years of cooking, barbecue pros have learned that making your ribs a little bit too tender and a little bit too sweet can get you a good score when they are judged.

Prepare your cooker to cook indirectly at 235°F using medium pecan wood for smoke flavor.

Peel the membrane off the back of the ribs and trim any excess fat. Season the ribs liberally on both sides with the rub. Place the ribs in the smoker, meat-side up, and cook for 2 hours. Flip the ribs and cook for 45 minutes.

Lay out two double-thick sheets of heavy-duty aluminum foil. Lay one slab on each piece of foil, meat-side up. Top each slab with half of the brown sugar. Drizzle each slab

2 slabs St. Louis–cut pork ribs (about 2½ pounds each)

Ray's Supersweet Rib Rub (page 31)

1 cup packed brown sugar

½ cup honey

¼ cup butter, melted

¼ cup Tiger Sauce or other pepper sauce that's not too vinegary

Thick and Rich Barbecue Sauce (page 38)

continued

with half of the honey, butter, and Tiger Sauce. Close up the rib packages, pressing out as much air as possible. Do not seal the packages tightly; they need to breathe a little..

Return to the cooker for 30 minutes. Open the packages and check for doneness by pushing a toothpick into the meat. It should go in and out very easily. If you want the ribs more tender, just wrap them back up and cook a little longer. When they're as you like them, transfer to a sheet pan. Remove the foil and return the ribs to the cooker, meat-side down. Brush the bone side liberally with barbecue sauce and cook for 10 minutes. Flip the ribs and brush the meat side liberally with barbecue sauce. Cook for 20 minutes. Transfer to a cutting board and tent loosely with foil. Let rest for 5 minutes. Slice each rib individually and transfer to a platter to serve.

COUNTRY-STYLE BARBECUED RIBS

MAKES
4 TO **6**
SERVINGS

Country-style ribs are a little different than spare-ribs or back ribs. You'll find some that are like pork chops and others that are from the shoulder. We're using the shoulder type for this recipe because they're easier to find. They're a little more economical than real ribs, but they're very good prepared this way and your friends and family will love them.

Trim any excess fat from the ribs. Season the ribs liberally with the rub. Cover and return to the refrigerator for at least 1 hour and up to 4 hours.

Prepare your cooker to cook indirectly at 235°F using a combination of two thirds cherry and one third hickory wood for smoke flavor. Put the ribs in the cooker with the fat side up where applicable. Cook for 3 hours.

Brush the ribs liberally with the barbecue sauce. Cook for 1 hour more, or until the ribs are very tender. Check for doneness by pushing a toothpick into the meaty part of a rib. It should go in and out very easily. Transfer to a platter, tent loosely with foil, and let rest for 6 minutes before serving.

4 pounds country-style pork ribs cut from the shoulder

Barbecue Rub #67 (page 29)

Thick and Rich Barbecue Sauce (page 38)

WINDY CITY RIB TIPS

MAKES ABOUT
6
SERVINGS

Barbecue Rub #67 (page 29)

Rib tips from 3 slabs of ribs
(about 3 pounds)

¾ cup Thick and Rich Barbecue
Sauce (page 38)

¾ cup apple juice

Rib tips are the cartilage section that's cut from the spareribs when making St. Louis–cut spareribs. They're not truly ribs and they require a little more work to cook. These have always been popular in Chicago, but lately the word has gotten out and now they're showing up all over the country. Tips are a little messier to eat than ribs; you really have to dig in, but the meat is as good or maybe even better.

Prepare your cooker to cook indirectly at 235°F using a combination of one third hickory and two thirds cherry wood for smoke flavor.

Apply a heavy coat of the rub to the tips and put them in the cooker for 3 hours. Remove from the cooker and cut across the length into pieces about 1½ inches long. Put all the pieces in an aluminum foil pan.

In a small bowl, whisk together the barbecue sauce and apple juice. Pour the mixture over the rib tips and toss well to coat. Cover the pan with aluminum foil and return to the cooker for another 1½ hours, until very tender to the touch. Serve immediately.

KOREAN-STYLE BARBECUE SHORT RIBS

MAKES **4** TO **6** SERVINGS

This is a nice smoker version of Korean-style short ribs. The smoking gives them a great flavor, while the cooking in the pan helps to tenderize. Be sure to get cross-cut (flaken style) ribs to enhance the taste from the marinade and for that great appearance. Once these are done, you might want to pull the meat off the bones and make some Korean tacos with it.

To make the marinade: In a medium bowl, combine the soy sauce, green onions, brown sugar, sesame oil, vinegar, garlic, ginger, chile, and sambal oelek. Mix well.

Put the short ribs in a gallon-size plastic zip bag. Pour the marinade over them and seal the bag, pushing out as much air as possible. Refrigerate, turning occasionally, for at least 2 hours but no longer than 4 hours.

Prepare your cooker to cook indirectly at 235°F using medium cherry or apple wood for smoke flavor. Take the ribs out of the marinade and put them directly on the cooking grate. Cook for 2 hours, until nicely browned.

continued

MARINADE

1 cup soy sauce

8 green onions, white and green parts thinly sliced

⅓ cup packed brown sugar

¼ cup sesame oil

¼ cup rice vinegar

6 large garlic cloves, crushed

2 tablespoons crushed peeled fresh ginger

1 serrano chile, minced

1 teaspoon sambal oelek (a spicy chili paste available in the Asian section of most markets)

3 pounds beef short ribs, cut across the bones flanken style about ½ inch thick

¼ cup apple juice

Meanwhile, pour the leftover marinade into a small saucepan and bring it to a simmer. Cook for 5 minutes and then remove it from the heat. Pour the marinade through a strainer. Reserve ¼ cup of the liquid and discard the rest. In a small bowl, combine the ¼ cup strained marinade with the apple juice. Mix well and set aside.

After the ribs have cooked for 2 hours, transfer them to a foil pan. Pour the juice mixture over them. Cover with foil and return to the cooker for another 2 hours, or until tender when squeezed between your fingers. Remove the pan from the cooker and let rest for 5 minutes. Transfer the ribs to a platter and pour any pan juices over the top. Serve immediately.

SMOKY BRAISED BEEF SHORT RIBS

8 beef short ribs, trimmed

Barbecue Rub #68 (page 30)

3 tablespoons olive oil

1 onion, chopped

2 stalks celery, chopped

1 green bell pepper, chopped

2 garlic cloves, chopped

1 cup red wine

1 cup beef stock

½ cup barbecue sauce

Salt

Black pepper

3 tablespoons cornstarch

Pork ribs are by far the most popular for barbecue, but beef ribs can be used, too. The meat is a little bit coarser and tougher, so a process like this with some braising helps to get them tender while keeping them juicy. And the smoking in the beginning gives them that great barbecue flavor. This is a perfect way to get started with beef ribs and guarantees that they'll be tender and juicy.

Prepare your cooker to cook indirectly at 235°F using medium pecan wood for smoke flavor.

Season the ribs liberally with the rub and place them in the smoker. Cook for 1½ hours.

Meanwhile, add the olive oil to a Dutch oven over medium heat. Add the onion, celery, bell pepper, and garlic and cook, stirring often, until the vegetables begin to soften. Add the wine, stock, and barbecue sauce and mix well. Bring to a simmer and cook for 5 minutes. Remove from the heat. Season with salt and pepper.

Preheat the oven or raise the temperature of your cooker to 325°F. When the ribs are finished smoking, transfer them to a 9-by-13-inch baking pan. Top with the vegetable mixture. Cover with foil and place in the cooker or oven. Cook for about 2 hours, or until tender to the touch. When the ribs are done, remove the bones and trim any loose ends. Transfer them to a pan and keep warm.

Strain the liquid from the pan and transfer it to a saucepan. Simmer to reduce by half. Thicken with a slurry of ¼ cup water mixed with the cornstarch. Cook until thickened.

Plate one or two short ribs, top with the sauce, and serve.

PORK, GLORIOUS PORK

Pork and barbecue. These two words go together like yin and yang. They complement each other like John and Paul or Beavis and Butthead. In just about every culture in the world, there is some celebratory ritual that involves whole hogs and fire. The size of the hog is just right for cooking in its entirety and the meat is a perfect match with fire—both in taste and texture. At home we don't generally attack the whole animal, but the parts work very well.

When you're shopping for pork, start by looking for a nice, even pink color throughout the meat. Pork doesn't get graded for quality by the USDA and frankly, almost all of it is top quality, but look for some marbled fat throughout the meat and a small amount around the outside. The tender and lean loin muscles of a hog are great as chops and roasts; the hams are legendary when cured and smoked; and the meat from the ribs is among the finest cuts a chef can cook. But for the barbecue man, the cuts that we dream about come from the shoulder. The slow cooking that is barbecue works best when the piece of meat is big and thick with a lot of fat, both on top and within. This perfectly describes a pork butt. And if you've ever had the pleasure of pulling a morsel of meat from a freshly cooked barbecued pork butt, you'll most likely agree that it's one of the best things you'll ever put in your mouth. The tender and juicy meat is just fatty enough to have an amazing mouthfeel with an incredible array of flavors. It's truly nirvana for a serious carnivore.

There is no doubt that beef brisket and ribs are also wonderful when smoked, but a pork butt is the class of the field and the clear favorite throughout the American South. You'll need to cook it a long time to get it right, like in the ten- to twelve-hour range, but that's what barbecue is all about. The spices and the smoke combine with the juices from the meat and as it slowly cooks it all caramelizes into a tasty, rich outside crust we call the "bark." At the same time, the fat is rendering and the inside meat is slow-cooking itself into a tender and juicy delicacy. When it's done, you remove the fat that's left and the bone and you pull the meat apart into shreds combining the soft inside meat with the highly flavored outside and the combination is just perfect. If you have never cooked a pork butt, please try it soon.

In just about every culture in the world, there is some celebratory ritual that involves whole hogs and fire.

The "butt" is actually the shoulder blade of the hog. The upper arm is called the picnic or picnic ham. The two cuts are sometimes cooked together as a whole shoulder. When this is done, the butt is the butt end of the shoulder and that's why it's called that. But for the home cook, a whole shoulder is a big cut of meat, like around twenty pounds big—so for most of us it's best to cook the parts individually. The picnic isn't as popular among barbecue guys as the butt, but it's equally good. It'll probably still have the skin on when you buy it but it's easily removed with a sharp knife. If you like more of a shank meat kind of flavor and texture, the picnic is a great choice. You'll find the yield to be a little less than a butt but other than that the two are interchangeable in any of my recipes. The cut that results from a pork butt that's sliced before cooking is known as pork shoulder steak. These cook well, and of course quicker than a whole butt, with the same great pork taste.

Pork and your barbecue cooker are going to get along very well.

The other cut of pork that is commonly used in barbecue is the loin. This is a much leaner cut than the shoulder but still very tasty, so it does very well on the smoker if you treat it right. I like to brine this cut to help keep it moist during the cooking and you'll see a couple recipes here that use the technique. I like to brine these things for a reasonably short amount of time, just to plump them up and add some great flavor. If you brine pork for too long, it changes to a firmer texture than I like, kind of like a ham. Quick brining

keeps the texture the same as fresh. I've also included a pork tenderloin recipe for a quick smoke, where we add a little smoke flavor without overcooking it. I've left pork ribs out of this chapter, mainly because they are so popular. They have their own whole chapter (see page 44).

Some general rules for cooking pork per the USDA are to always cook it to an internal temperature of 145°F. I'll sort of go along with that for the lean cuts like loin and tenderloin, although I might prefer 150°F. We all know that today's pork is safe, juicy, and tender when it's served a little bit pink. But barbecue cuts like the butts and picnic are a little different. At 145°F they'd still be a little tough and the fat wouldn't be rendered as much as we like. The general rule of thumb is to cook those cuts to an internal temperature of 195° to 200°F for pork that will pull apart, and that's what makes real barbecue. So pick the right cut and the right recipes and get cooking! Pork and your barbecue cooker are going to get along very well.

LOW AND SLOW MEMPHIS-STYLE PULLED PORK

Slow-smoked pork shoulder is what real barbecue is all about in Memphis—long shreds of meat served with a little barbecue sauce on the side as a main course or a great sandwich. It's a good choice for the new barbecue cook to try, too, because it's a little more forgiving than some of the other cuts if you don't get it just right. Just make sure to start early and cook it until it's done. It may seem like a long time, but the results are well worth it.

Do not trim the fat cap off the pork butt! You may trim any extra pieces that are hanging loose, but most of the trimming will be done after the cooking. Season the meat liberally with the rub. Put it in the refrigerator for at least 30 minutes and up to 4 hours.

One 7- to 8-pound pork butt

Barbecue Rub #67 (page 29)

½ cup apple juice

Barbecue sauce

continued

Prepare your cooker to cook indirectly at 235°F using a combination of two thirds cherry and one third hickory wood for smoke flavor. Put the butt in the cooker, fat-side up, and cook until the internal temperature is 180°F. This should take 8 to 10 hours, depending on your cooker.

Lay out a big double-thick sheet of heavy-duty aluminum foil and put the pork butt in the middle. As you begin to close up the package, pour the apple juice over the top of the butt and then seal the package, taking care not to puncture it. Put the package back in the cooker until the thickest part of the meat reaches an internal temperature of 200°F. This should take about another 2 hours.

Transfer the package from the cooker to a sheet pan. Open the top of the foil to let the steam out and let it rest for 30 minutes. Using heavy insulated gloves or a pair of tongs and a fork, transfer the meat to a big pan. It will be very tender and hard to handle. Discard the juices as they will be quite fatty. Pull the meat apart with your hands, discarding the fat and bones. Keep in big chunks or continue pulling into shreds if you prefer. Serve immediately with barbecue sauce on the side.

COMPETITION-STYLE PORK BUTT

PORK INJECTION

1 cup apple juice

½ cup pineapple juice

½ cup packed brown sugar

¼ cup salt

2 tablespoons Worcestershire sauce

2 tablespoons soy sauce

2 tablespoons hot sauce

½ teaspoon cayenne pepper

One 8-pound pork butt

Barbecue Rub #67 (page 29)

Barbecue sauce

The big-time barbecue cook-off guys do some things that are pretty ambitious for the home cook. But they need to because the judges will critique them after just one or two bites, so their food needs to pack a wallop. Injecting pork butts is something that most of them do and, while it adds great flavor all the way through the butt, it really doesn't overpower the pork flavor. You'll need to get a kitchen injector, available at just about any kitchen store and most supermarkets. The process is simple—just don't add anything chunky to the liquid or it won't work because the needle has a small hole.

A few hours before you plan to cook, make the injection: In a medium saucepan over medium heat, combine the apple juice, pineapple juice, brown sugar, ¼ cup water, the salt, Worcestershire, soy sauce, hot sauce, and cayenne. Cook for 5 minutes, stirring often, until the salt and sugar are mixed in. Refrigerate and cool completely. The liquid must be cold before you inject it.

Cover the meat loosely with plastic wrap and wear an apron; this can get a little messy. With a kitchen injector, inject 1½ cups of the injection liquid into the pork butt by poking the needle in a grid pattern 2 inches deep and 1 inch apart and squeezing a small amount into each hole, about 1 tablespoon. Rub the meat liberally with the rub. Place the butt in a pan. Cover with plastic wrap and refrigerate for at least 30 minutes and up to 8 hours.

Prepare your cooker to cook indirectly at 235°F using a combination of two thirds cherry and one third hickory wood for smoke flavor. Put the butt in the cooker and cook until the internal temperature reaches 160°F, about 8 hours.

Lay out a big double-thick sheet of heavy-duty aluminum foil and put the pork butt in the middle. As you begin to close up the package, pour the last ½ cup of injection liquid over the top of the butt and then seal the package, taking care not to puncture it. Put the package back in the cooker until the thickest part of the meat reaches an internal temperature of 200°F. This should take another 3 to 4 hours.

Transfer the package from the cooker to a sheet pan. Open the top of the foil to let the steam out and let it rest for 30 minutes. Using heavy insulated gloves, pull the meat apart in big chunks, discarding the bone and all the fat. Brush the big pretty chunks lightly with barbecue sauce and then set them aside. Shred the smaller pieces with your hands and toss them with a little more rub and a small amount of barbecue sauce. Lay out a bed of the shredded meat and lay the big chunks on top to serve.

1 fresh 6-pound pork picnic leg

2 tablespoons olive oil

Dr. BBQ's Fired-Up Fajita Rub
(page 34)

SPICY SMOKED PORK PICNIC

The picnic is the front arm of the hog and it's a great-tasting cut of pork. It can be used interchangeably with the pork butt, but the picnic is a little fattier and a little more hamlike—both in taste and texture. Even if you prefer the butt, the picnic is a nice option when you're looking for a little change of pace. In barbecue, we cook it until it's tender enough to pull from the bone, and with a spicy rub it's something very special.

With a sharp, thin knife, remove the skin from the pork leg, leaving the fat intact. Cut a series of shallow slashes about 1 inch apart all over the meat in a crosshatch pattern. Rub the pork with the olive oil and season liberally with the rub. Cover with plastic wrap and refrigerate for 1 hour.

Prepare your cooker to cook indirectly at 235°F using medium pecan wood for smoke flavor. Place the pork in the cooker, fatty-side up, and cook until the internal temperature reaches 165°F, about 6 hours. Remove the pork from the cooker and wrap it tightly in aluminum foil. Return to the cooker until the internal temperature reaches 190°F, about 2 more hours.

Transfer the pork to a platter and open the foil a little to let the steam out and let it rest for 15 minutes. Slice the meat off the bone to serve.

CUBAN-STYLE LEG OF PORK

MAKES 12 SERVINGS

This is a very popular dish in Florida, where Cuban and Spanish influence on the food abounds. The sour orange juice is really unique and the key to this dish. If it's not available to you locally, look around on the Internet. It may seem like you use a lot of salt here, but that is also a key to the authentic flavor. It's a simple prep—just make sure you get it marinating a day ahead of cooking. This dish should always be served with black beans and rice.

With a sharp, thin knife, remove the skin from the pork leg, leaving the fat intact. Stab the pork leg deeply in an X fashion every couple inches on all sides.

Put the garlic in the bowl of a food processor fitted with a metal blade. In a medium bowl, mix together the orange juice, salt, olive oil, cumin, oregano, and pepper. Pour the mixture over the garlic. Process on high for about 20 seconds, until the mixture is well blended. Transfer the paste mixture to a small bowl. Rub the paste mixture all over the leg, shoving

continued

1 fresh 8-pound pork picnic leg

15 garlic cloves, coarsely chopped

¼ cup sour orange juice (or 3 tablespoons orange juice and 1 tablespoon lime juice)

¼ cup kosher salt

2 tablespoons olive oil

1 tablespoon ground cumin

1 tablespoon dried oregano

1 teaspoon black pepper

1 onion, thinly sliced

MOJO

2 tablespoons olive oil

6 garlic cloves, crushed

1 teaspoon salt

1 teaspoon black pepper

1 teaspoon ground cumin

1 teaspoon dried oregano

1 cup sour orange juice (or ¾ cup orange juice and ¼ cup lime juice)

it deeply into all of the holes. Put the leg in a large plastic bag and toss in the onion, spreading it evenly around the leg. Seal the bag and refrigerate for at least 12 hours and preferably 24.

Prepare your cooker to cook indirectly at 235°F using mild pecan wood for smoke flavor. Take the pork leg out of the bag and place it, fat-side up, in an aluminum foil pan. Place the pan in the cooker for 2 hours. Flip the leg over and cook for 2 hours more.

Meanwhile, make the mojo: Heat the olive oil in a small saucepan over medium heat. Add the garlic and cook, stirring often, for 2 minutes. Add the salt, pepper, cumin, and oregano and cook for 3 minutes, stirring often. Add the orange juice and stir well. Remove from the heat and set aside.

Flip the leg again and baste with half of the mojo. Cook for 30 minutes. Flip the leg and baste with the remaining mojo. Cook for 30 minutes. Flip the leg again and cover the pan with aluminum foil. Continue cooking until the internal temperature of the meat reaches 195°F, about 3 to 4 hours more.

Remove the pan and transfer the leg to a platter. Tent it loosely with foil and let it rest for 15 minutes. Transfer the liquid from the pan to a bowl or large pitcher. Let it rest, then skim off as much grease as possible. Pull the roast off the bones in chunks and transfer them to a platter, discarding all the bones and fat. Serve with the mojo on the side as a sauce.

BACON-WRAPPED PIG WINGS

MAKES
12
SERVINGS

Who says pigs can't fly? Take a few boneless pork chops, add some bacon and a little creativity, and Pig Wings are on the menu! The bacon adds great flavor and keeps the loin meat from getting dry. These look delicious and are a little unusual, so they make a fabulous smoked appetizer with barbecue sauce for dipping. The kids will love them.

Cut each pork chop into three strips. To wrap the "wings," start by overlapping the bacon on one end of a pork strip, then wrapping it up and around in a candy-cane fashion. Secure the bacon at the top with a toothpick. If you need to use a toothpick at both ends, go ahead. Season the bacon-wrapped wings liberally with the rub.

Prepare your cooker to cook indirectly at 235°F using medium pecan wood for smoke flavor. Place the wings directly on the cooking grid and cook for 90 minutes, or until the bacon is done. You may want to finish these on a hot grill or under the broiler to crisp the bacon. Serve hot with barbecue sauce for dipping.

Four 1-inch-thick boneless pork chops

12 slices bacon (do not use thick sliced)

Barbecue Rub #67 (page 29)

Barbecue sauce, for dipping

SLICED PORK SHOULDER ROAST

1 boneless pork shoulder roast (about 5 pounds)

2 garlic cloves, cut into slivers

2 tablespoons olive oil

Barbecue Rub #68 (page 30)

There is more than one way to barbecue a pork butt. While many of us like it cooked to the point of pulling apart, it's also quite good cooked a little less and sliced. For this recipe, you'll need a pork shoulder roast. It's really just a boneless pork butt with the fat cap removed, and then it's rolled and tied. If you don't see it at the market, ask the butcher and he'll know what you want.

Prepare your cooker to cook indirectly at 235°F using mild pecan wood for smoke flavor.

With a long, pointy knife, stab the roast deeply every few inches. Stick a sliver of garlic in each of the holes. Brush the roast all over with the olive oil. Season the roast liberally with the rub. Put the roast in the cooker. Cook until the internal temperature reaches 180°F, about 6 hours.

Transfer the roast to a platter and tent loosely with foil. Let rest for 10 minutes. Slice the meat thinly to serve.

SMOKED MAPLE-BRINED PORK CHOPS

MAKES
4
SERVINGS

Short-term brining like this works very well for adding flavor to the meat and helping it to stay juicy without the texture changes that can happen with long-term brining. It's a simple technique, but really helpful with smaller cuts for the barbecue beginner. Smoked pork chops with the flavor addition of maple are a favorite cut for lunch and dinner, but also taste great refried and served with eggs for breakfast.

To make the brine: At least 5 hours before you plan to cook, heat I cup of water in a small saucepan over medium heat. When the water begins to simmer, add the maple syrup, salt, mustard powder, cayenne, and cinnamon. Mix well, and when the salt has dissolved, remove from the heat. Transfer the brine to a bowl and add the ice water. Refrigerate for at least 30 minutes, until very cold.

Place the chops in a gallon-size plastic zip bag and add the cold brine. Press out as much air as possible and seal the bag. Refrigerate for 4 hours, turning occasionally.

Prepare your cooker to cook indirectly at 235°F using medium cherry wood for smoke flavor.

Remove the chops from the brine and discard the brine. Rinse well and dry the chops with paper towels. Season lightly on both sides with the chili powder and place the chops in the smoker. Cook until they reach an internal temperature of 145°F, about I hour. Transfer to a platter and tent loosely with foil. Let rest for 5 minutes. Drizzle lightly with maple syrup to serve.

BRINE

3 tablespoons maple syrup

2 tablespoons kosher salt

¼ teaspoon dry mustard powder

¼ teaspoon cayenne

⅛ teaspoon ground cinnamon

1 cup ice water

4 boneless pork loin chops, about 1¼ inches thick

Chili powder

Maple syrup

BRINE

2 tablespoons kosher salt

1 tablespoon honey

1 teaspoon brown sugar

1 teaspoon Louisiana hot sauce

½ teaspoon black pepper

1 cup ice water

1 boneless center-cut pork loin roast (about 2½ pounds)

Barbecue Rub #68 (page 30)

Banana Ketchup (page 43)

SMOKED PORK LOIN WITH BANANA KETCHUP

Boneless pork loin, also known as "the Other White Meat," is a tender and tasty cut. But it's a lean cut, so it's not the best choice for smoking unless we help it out a little. A simple brine like this one keeps it moist and juicy while adding some terrific flavor that matches well with my version of banana ketchup. This dish is perfect for Sunday dinner and then makes great sandwiches for lunch during the week.

To make the brine: At least 5 hours before you plan to cook, heat 1 cup of water in a small saucepan over medium heat. When the water begins to simmer, add the salt, honey, brown sugar, hot sauce, and pepper. Mix well, and when the salt has dissolved, remove from the heat. Transfer the brine to a bowl and add the ice water. Refrigerate for at least 30 minutes, until very cold.

Cut very shallow slashes in the top and bottom of the roast in an angled X pattern. Place the roast in a heavy-plastic zip bag and add the cold brine. Press out as much air as possible and seal the bag. Refrigerate for 4 hours, turning occasionally.

Prepare your cooker to cook indirectly at 235°F using medium apple wood for smoke flavor.

Remove the pork from the brine and discard the brine. Rinse the roast well and dry it with paper towels. Season liberally with the rub and place it in the smoker. Cook until it reaches an internal temp of 150°F, about 2 hours.

Remove the pork from the cooker and wrap it tightly in foil. Let rest for 15 minutes. Slice and serve with the banana ketchup on the side.

SMOKED PORK STEAKS WITH WHISKEY ONIONS

MAKES
4
SERVINGS

Pork steaks are slices of pork butt and a really tasty cut for the grill or smoker. They're a good bargain, too, when you've got a crowd to feed. It's kind of a grown-up pork chop taste that goes well with many fun flavors after a little bit of smoking. For this dish I chose whiskey and onions, which are a great combo, but feel free to tweak this one any way you like.

Prepare your cooker to cook indirectly at 235°F using medium apple wood for smoke flavor.

Season the pork steaks liberally with the rub and put them in the cooker. Cook for 2 hours, then remove them from the cooker and lay them in a shingle fashion in an aluminum foil pan. Top with the sliced onion. Season the onion lightly with salt and a little more rub. Splash the whiskey over the onion. Cover with aluminum foil and return to the cooker for 2 hours more, until the meat is tender when squeezed between your fingers.

Remove the pan from the cooker and carefully transfer the steaks to a platter; they will be very tender. Top with the onion to serve.

4 pork shoulder steaks (about 3 pounds total)

Barbecue Rub #68 (page 30)

1 large red onion, halved and very thinly sliced

Salt

¼ cup Jack Daniel's Whiskey

CILANTRO-SMEARED PORK TENDERLOIN

2 whole pork tenderloins
(about 2½ pounds total)

1 bunch fresh cilantro

¼ cup olive oil

3 garlic cloves, crushed

1 jalapeño, minced (remove
the seeds if you don't like a
little heat)

Juice of 1 lime

1 teaspoon salt

½ teaspoon black pepper

Pork tenderloin is very lean, and because of that we don't usually think of it as a typical barbecue meat. But with the added flavor from the cilantro smear and a quick smoke, it's a tasty and unique offering from the smoker. It's a great way to have real barbecue when you don't have all day to cook. The color will be lighter than most of the meats from your smoker, but that's fine. As with any lean pork, just don't overcook it!

Trim all the fat and silverskin from the pork tenderloins. In the bowl of a food processor fitted with a metal blade, combine the cilantro, olive oil, garlic, jalapeño, lime juice, salt, and pepper. Pulse a few times, scrape down the sides, and pulse again, until the mixture is well combined and resembles a pesto. Rub the cilantro mixture all over the pork. Refrigerate for at least 1 hour and up to 4 hours.

Prepare your cooker to cook indirectly at 235°F using medium cherry wood for smoke flavor. Put the pork in the cooker and cook until it reaches an internal temperature of 150°F, about 1½ hours.

Transfer the pork to a platter and tent loosely with aluminum foil. Let rest 5 minutes. Slice to serve.

DOUBLE-SMOKED HAM WITH APRICOT GLAZE

A ham may be fully cooked and usually smoked as well, but another round in the smoker and a tasty glaze really take it to the next level. The apricot-soy combo here adds a sweet/salty taste to the outside of the ham. This recipe calls for a bone-in ham, but you can easily adapt it to any cooked ham. This is a great way to impress the family for the holidays and leave the oven available for other dishes.

Prepare your cooker to cook indirectly at 235°F using medium hickory wood for smoke flavor.

Lay the ham cut-side down on a cutting board. With a sharp knife, score the skin in a diamond pattern on all sides. Place the ham in the cooker with the cut side down and cook for 2 hours.

To make the glaze: In the large bowl of a food processor fitted with a metal blade, combine the apricots, ketchup, soy sauce, and molasses. Process for about 15 seconds, until the mixture is smooth. Transfer the glaze to a bowl and set aside.

After the ham has cooked for 2 hours, brush it all over with a heavy coating of the glaze. Cook for 30 minutes and glaze the ham again. Cook for an additional 30 minutes.

Transfer the ham to a platter and tent loosely with aluminum foil. Let rest for 15 minutes. Slice to serve.

1 semi-boneless fully cooked ham (6 to 7 pounds)

GLAZE

One 15-ounce can apricot halves in heavy syrup, drained

¼ cup ketchup

2 tablespoons soy sauce

1 tablespoon molasses

CHAPTER 4

BEAUTIFUL BEEF

Beef is always a great choice for low and slow barbecue. A tender, juicy brisket is a barbecue classic, but don't overlook some of your other favorite cuts. The big flavor of beef always pairs well with a little smoke. But when choosing beef, there's more to know than simply the cut you want to use. Beef, unlike pork and chicken, is regularly graded for quality by the United States Department of Agriculture (USDA). The grades are based largely on the quantity of marbling or internal fat content, which is what makes the beef tender and tasty.

The three USDA grades you'll regularly find at retail are Select, Choice, and Prime. USDA Select is very lean and it can be tough. Sometimes a fatty cut such as a rib eye is acceptable, but for most of us USDA Select graded beef is not a very good choice. The next grade, and by far the most common, is USDA Choice. It has enough marbling to be tender and juicy and the price is acceptable to most home cooks. The last, and highest, grade is USDA Prime. This is what you find at the fancy steak houses. It's heavily marbled, making it tender, juicy, and delicious. The cattle that produce USDA Prime meat are fed a high-quality feed and they are very well cared for, but that also makes them expensive.

There's one last option and it has become very popular with the big boys of the barbecue world. It's Wagyu. Wagyu is the breed of cattle used to produce the legendary Kobe beef from Japan. It's unlikely that you'll find real Japanese Kobe beef in the United States, but you can find the American version, simply called Wagyu. It's very good, claiming to grade above USDA Prime. You won't find it at the supermarket, but you might find it at a high-end butcher shop. It's also available on the Internet and can be shipped to your house. A great source is Snake River Farms from Idaho. Choose what fits your taste and budget, but in most cases USDA Choice beef is the best for barbecue.

In the great tradition of barbecue, where the less desirable cuts worked their way into the barbecue pit, brisket fits the bill.

Beef is the favored meat for barbecue in the regions where they have a lot of cattle, like Kansas City, Oklahoma, and, of course, Texas. No surprise there, and the favorite cut of beef for slow smoking is always the brisket. In the great tradition of barbecue, where the less desirable cuts worked their way into the barbecue pit, brisket fits the bill. It's a big, lean, tough cut of meat and if you don't cook it right it's pretty much inedible. But when you do cook it right, all the collagen breaks down and the meat is tender and moist and has a great beefy flavor.

A whole brisket, also known as a packer cut brisket, is a big piece of meat. Look for one that weighs at least twelve pounds and has a lot of fat on top. We call this the "fat cap," and it's essential for cooking a brisket properly.

A whole brisket consists of two very distinct muscles and a lot of fat and that's what makes it a perfect candidate for long, slow cooking in the barbecue pit. The flat muscle has a tight grain much like a flank steak, but it's much tougher and much leaner. Slow and low cooking is best so it won't dry out while it cooks its way to tenderness. The point muscle is quite different, with a looser grain and a lot of marbling fat throughout. But it's also very tough and requires long, slow cooking to render the fat while it becomes tender. So while these muscles are very different, they cook well together and the point muscle even acts as a natural baster for the flat as the fat renders from one muscle to the other.

The basic cooking concept for a brisket is to leave all the fat on, season it heavily, and slow-smoke it for many hours, until the internal temperature reaches about 200°F. If you just can't wait it out, wrapping it in foil once the internal temperature gets above 170°F is acceptable. This will hurry it up a little and may keep it from drying out at the end. Once cooked, the muscles should be separated and the fat trimmed and discarded. The flat muscle then slices beautifully for sandwiches, while the point muscle is best served chopped or cut into cubes to be served as burnt ends. You will often see the flat muscle by itself available at the store and it cooks nicely as long as they haven't trimmed all the fat away. When choosing a brisket flat, look for one that's at least five pounds, with a nice layer of fat on top. Anything smaller or trimmed of fat really won't cook like a real brisket, so don't even bother with it. The point muscle isn't readily available on its own, although it's mighty tasty and I often wish it was!

While brisket is king and there are a few good ways to cook it, there are other cuts of beef that work well on the barbecue pit, too. Keep in mind that fat is a good thing for long, slow cooking. That's why I like prime rib, chuck roasts, and dishes made with ground beef. I've also included a recipe for a sirloin tip roast. While it's a lean cut, it still works well on the smoker as long as you serve it medium-rare. Be careful not to overcook it and it will be great. Whichever cut you choose, beef in the barbecue pit is always a good thing.

PULLED BARBECUE BEEF

It's called "pulled" beef because it's cooked until the meat is tender enough to pull into shreds with your hands. This dish is smoky, tender, and juicy, with a little onion and barbecue sauce flavor—kind of like big-time sloppy joes. Just make sure to cook it all the way until it's falling-apart tender. Of course it makes for great sandwiches, but you might also try using it for tacos, over noodles, or even on pizza.

Prepare your cooker to cook indirectly at 235°F using medium oak wood for smoke flavor.

Season the roast liberally with the rub, patting it to adhere to the meat. Let rest for 15 minutes at room temperature. Put the roast in the cooker and cook for 3 hours.

Remove the roast and put it in a medium aluminum foil pan. Pour the broth over the roast. Top the roast with the sliced onion. Sprinkle a little more rub on the onion. Cover with foil and return to the cooker. Cook for 3 hours, or until the roast is fork-tender.

Uncover the pan and push the onion off the top of the roast into the drippings. Remove the roast from the pan and shred it with two forks. If there are some tough parts, use a knife to slice them thinly. Add the barbecue sauce to the drippings and mix well. Add the meat back to the pan and toss well with the liquid. Cover with foil. Return to the cooker for 1 hour. Remove from the cooker and toss the meat with the juices to mix well before serving.

1 USDA Choice boneless chuck roast (about 4 pounds)

Barbecue Rub #67 (page 29)

½ cup low-sodium beef broth

1 yellow onion, halved and sliced thinly

1 cup barbecue sauce

¼ cup Barbecue Rub #67 (page 29)

¼ cup Dr. BBQ's Fired-Up Fajita Rub (page 34)

1 USDA Choice whole brisket (about 12 pounds)

Three 12-ounce cans beer, preferably Lone Star

REAL TEXAS-STYLE BEEF BRISKET

Cooking brisket is a challenge for the beginning barbecue chef, so this may not be the best place to start. But once you are comfortable with your cooker and your meat thermometer, give it a go. There is no better eating than barbecued brisket. A real Texas brisket is always a whole brisket cooked with most of the fat intact. It's seasoned with something simple and a little spicy and then cooked for a long time over oak wood. The traditional accompaniments are sliced raw onion, pickles, and jalapeños. Hot sauce is often used as well, but traditional barbecue sauce is not.

In a small bowl, mix together the two rubs.

Prepare your cooker to cook indirectly at 235°F using oak wood for smoke flavor.

Trim most of the fat from the pockets on the sides of the brisket. Then cut along the outside edge where needed to get rid of any loose pieces. The fat cap should remain mostly intact. If there is an extremely thick spot, trim it to even things out.

Wet the whole brisket with half of one beer. Season all the
exposed meat liberally with the mixed rubs. (Drink the other
half of the beer.) Place the brisket in the smoker, fat-side
down. Cook for 4 hours. Pour half of another beer on the
brisket and cook another 4 hours. (Drink the other half of
the beer.) Pour half of the third beer on the brisket and flip
to cook it fat-side up. (Drink the other half of the beer.) Cook
until the brisket is tender when you stab it with a skewer.
This should take about another 4 hours and the internal
temperature should reach 195°F.

Wrap the brisket in foil and transfer it to an empty ice chest.
Top with a lot of crumpled newspapers to help keep it hot.
Let the brisket rest for 2 hours minimum and up to 4 hours.
Transfer to a cutting board and trim away all the fat. Slice the
brisket through both muscles across the grain about ⅜ inch
thick. Serve immediately.

MAKES ABOUT

15

SERVINGS

INJECTION LIQUID

2 cups beef broth

¼ cup Worcestershire sauce

1 teaspoon onion powder

1 teaspoon garlic powder

½ teaspoon cayenne pepper

1 USDA Choice whole brisket
(12 to 15 pounds)

Barbecue Rub #67 (page 29)

Thin and Spicy Barbecue Sauce
(page 39)

COMPETITION-STYLE BEEF BRISKET

The big-time cook-off guys do some pretty extreme things to get the attention of the judges. One thing almost all of the top cooks do is inject their briskets with a flavorful liquid before cooking. You'll need a kitchen injector, which is available at any kitchen store and most supermarkets. The flavor and moisture that it adds make for a great first bite of brisket when the judge digs in. For the home cook, it's a little more work but the results are pretty good. Injecting will help keep the brisket from drying out but it won't save an overcooked brisket. Be sure to check the temperature often with your meat thermometer to get it done just right.

To make the injection liquid: Combine the broth, Worcestershire, onion powder, garlic powder, and cayenne in a medium bowl. Mix well and refrigerate until cold.

Trim most of the fat from the pockets on the sides of the brisket. Then cut along the outside edge where needed to get rid of any loose pieces. The fat cap should remain mostly intact. If there is an extremely thick spot, trim it to even things out.

About 1 hour before you plan to cook, cover the brisket loosely with plastic wrap. With a kitchen injector, inject the brisket with the liquid in a grid pattern, injecting about 2 tablespoons every couple of inches.

Keep injecting until you've used all of the liquid. Dry the outside with a paper towel and season liberally with the rub on all sides. Let rest at room temperature for 30 minutes.

Prepare your cooker to cook indirectly at 235°F using half cherry and half oak wood for smoke flavor.

Place the brisket in the cooker, fat-side down. After 5 hours, flip the brisket over and continue cooking until the internal temperature reaches 180°F deep in the flat muscle. Lay out a double-thick layer of wide heavy-duty aluminum foil and place the brisket on it fat-side up. Wrap it up tightly and place it back in the cooker for about 2 hours, until the internal temperature deep in the flat muscle reaches 200°F and a skewer pushed into the meat slides in and out very easily.

Transfer the brisket to a large cutting board. Cool the liquid that has accumulated in the foil. Skim the fat and set it aside. Take a long carving knife and separate the two muscles, being very careful not to cut into either one. Trim all the fat from the point muscle. Season it again with the rub wherever it has been cut and return it to the cooker. Wrap the flat tightly in a double-thick sheet of heavy-duty aluminum foil and put it in an empty ice chest to hold. Top with crumpled newspapers to help keep it hot. It will stay hot for at least 4 hours this way.

Cook the point until it reaches an internal temp of 200°F and a skewer pushed into the meat slides in and out very easily. The time for this step will vary widely depending on your cooker but should be from 1 to 3 hours. When it's done, cut the point into cubes about 1½ inches square. In a large bowl, toss the cubes with the reserved liquid from the foil and a small amount of barbecue sauce.

Remove the flat from the foil and trim away all the fat. Slice across the grain about the thickness of a pencil and serve. At home, I prefer to serve the sauce on the side but at a cook-off I always brush each slice with barbecue sauce and I always turn in enough of the sliced and the burnt ends for each of the judges.

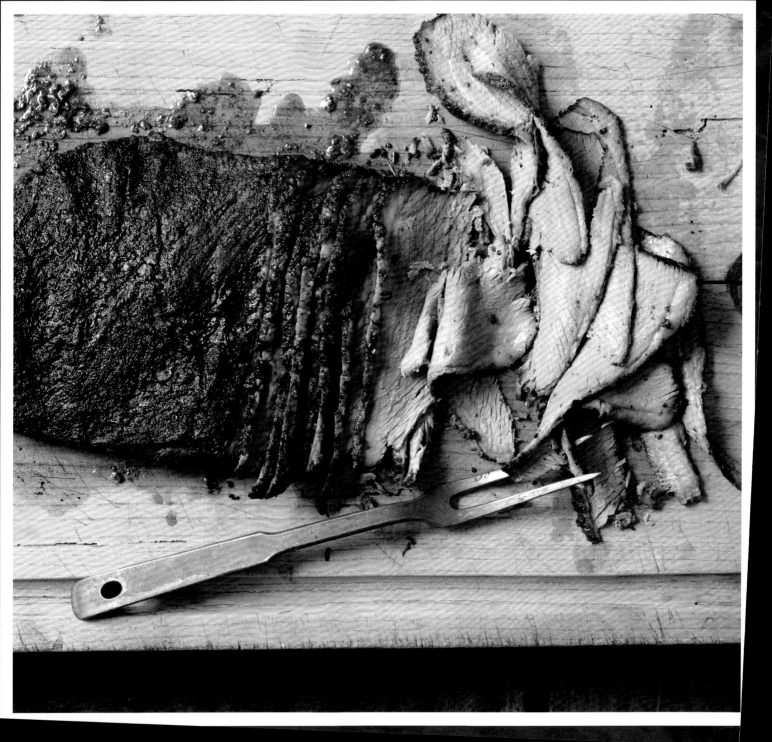

SMOKED FLAT-CUT BRISKET WITH COFFEE

The flat cut of brisket makes for those long, beautiful slices that look so good on the plate. This cut has a lot less fat on it than a whole brisket, though, so it needs a little added moisture during the cooking process. Coffee adds an interesting flavor while helping keep things juicy. A brisket flat is a simpler piece of meat to cook than a big whole brisket so this is probably a good place to start for a new barbecue cook. Just don't get one any smaller than 5 pounds.

Prepare your cooker to cook indirectly at 235°F using medium hickory wood for smoke flavor.

Season the brisket liberally with the rub. Cook the brisket fat-side down for 1 hour and then flip it to fat-side up. Cook to an internal temperature of 160°F, about another 3 to 4 hours.

Lay out a big double-thick layer of heavy-duty aluminum foil and lay the brisket on it fat-side up. Pull up the sides of the foil and pour on the coffee as you close up the package. Be careful not to puncture it or you'll have to start over. Return the brisket to the cooker. After another hour, begin checking the internal temperature. When it reaches 200°F, remove the brisket and let it rest for 30 minutes, wrapped. Remove the brisket from the foil. If desired, skim the fat from the liquid and serve the remaining juices as a sauce. Slice the brisket about ¼ inch thick to serve.

1 USDA Choice flat-cut brisket (5 to 6 pounds), fat left on

Barbecue Rub #67 (page 29)

½ cup strong brewed coffee

HOMEMADE PASTRAMI

BRINE INJECTION

2 tablespoons Morton's
Tender Quick

1 tablespoon brown sugar

2 teaspoons garlic powder

1 teaspoon ground coriander

½ teaspoon black pepper

1 cup ice water

DRY CURE

2 tablespoons Morton's
Tender Quick

2 tablespoons brown sugar

1½ tablespoons garlic powder

1 tablespoon ground coriander

1 USDA Choice flat-cut brisket
(about 7 pounds), fat left on

COOKING RUB

¼ cup coarsely ground
black pepper

3 tablespoons ground coriander

Everybody loves pastrami and this homemade version may be the best you've ever tasted. The recipe avoids the long brine method and substitutes a more efficient combination of injecting and dry-curing. It may seem like an intimidating project, but it's really pretty simple as long as you remember to start the process four days before you plan to eat it. If you can't find the Morton's Tender Quick near the salt at your local grocery store, look for it online.

To make the brine injection: In a small saucepan over medium heat, combine I cup of water, the Tender Quick, brown sugar, garlic powder, coriander, and pepper. Bring to a simmer, stirring often to dissolve the sugar. Remove from the heat and pour into a medium bowl. Add the ice water and mix well. Refrigerate until very cold.

To make the dry cure: In a small bowl, combine the Tender Quick, brown sugar, garlic powder, and coriander. Mix well and set aside.

Lay the brisket fat-side down on a sheet pan with sides. Cover loosely with plastic wrap. With a kitchen injector, inject the brine deeply into the brisket in a grid pattern at I-inch intervals. Continue until all of the brine has been used. Remove the plastic and dry the brisket and the pan. Flip the brisket over and season the fat side with half of the dry cure mixture. Press the mixture into the fat. Flip the brisket and season the other side

continued

with the remaining dry cure and press it into the meat. Put the brisket in a heavy plastic bag. Push out as much air as possible and seal the bag. Refrigerate for 3½ days, flipping and massaging it through the bag twice a day.

Take the brisket out of the bag and rinse it well under cold running water. Place the brisket in a large pan of cold water to cover for 30 minutes. Dump the water and replace it with fresh water; soak for another 30 minutes. This will keep the pastrami from being too salty.

Prepare your cooker to cook indirectly at 235°F using medium oak wood for smoke flavor.

To make the cooking rub: Combine the pepper and coriander in a small bowl and mix well.

Take the brisket out of the water and dry it well. Season the fat side with half of the cooking rub, pressing it into the meat. Flip the brisket and season the meaty side with the other half of the rub, pushing it into the meat. Put the brisket in the cooker, fat-side up. Cook for 4 hours and then flip the brisket to fat-side down. Cook until it reaches an internal temperature of 170°F, another 1 or 2 hours.

Lay out a big double-thick piece of heavy-duty aluminum foil. Take the brisket out of the cooker, and lay it on the foil fat-side up. Wrap the foil up around the brisket, adding ½ cup water to the package. Close up the package tightly, pushing out as much air as possible. Return to the cooker until the internal temperature of the brisket reaches 200°F, another 1 to 2 hours.

Take the package out of the cooker and open it to allow the steam to escape. Let rest for 15 minutes. Take the brisket out of the foil and discard the juices. Slice thinly across the grain to serve.

SMOKY ROAST BEEF AU MUSHROOM JUS

A simple beef roast becomes a very special dish when you cook it in the smoker. The great beefy taste of sirloin picks up the smoke flavor beautifully, even in a short cook like this. Add in the great taste of the barbecue rub and the mushroom jus and you may never cook your roast beef in the oven again.

Prepare your cooker to cook indirectly at 235°F using medium cherry wood for smoke flavor.

Season the roast liberally with the rub and refrigerate for 30 minutes.

To make the jus: In a large skillet over medium-high heat, melt the butter. Add the olive oil and then the mushrooms. Toss well to coat and cook for 3 minutes. Add the garlic, salt, and pepper. Mix well and cook for 5 minutes, stirring often, until the mushrooms begin to soften. Add the broth and bring to a simmer. Transfer the contents to a foil pan.

Put the roast and the mushroom mixture in the cooker side by side. After I hour, remove the pan of mushroom jus. Transfer it to a medium saucepan. Cover and set aside. Cook the roast until it reaches an internal temperature of I35°F, about 3 hours total.

Transfer the roast to a platter and tent it loosely with foil. Let the roast rest for I0 minutes. Place the pan of mushrooms over medium heat and bring them to a simmer. Transfer them to a serving bowl. Slice the roast thinly to serve with the mushroom jus on the side.

1 USDA Choice sirloin tip roast (4 to 5 pounds)

Barbecue Rub #68 (page 30)

MUSHROOM JUS

2 tablespoons butter

2 tablespoons olive oil

1 pound button mushrooms, quartered

3 garlic cloves, crushed

½ teaspoon salt

½ teaspoon black pepper

1 cup good-quality beef broth

SMOKED HOLIDAY PRIME RIB

MAKES
6 TO 8
SERVINGS

Prime rib is a big, impressive meal to serve at home and that's why so many of us serve it at holiday time. Smoking makes it even better and frees up the oven for all the great side dishes and desserts. I prefer a boneless roast, but some like the bones left on. You'll need to adjust your cooking times if you have bones, but the desired internal temperature will stay the same. Try serving this with the meat juices mixed with a little barbecue sauce and horseradish.

Wet the roast all over with the Worcestershire. Season it liberally with the rub, patting it on so it sticks to the meat. Let the meat rest at room temperature for 30 minutes.

Prepare your cooker to cook indirectly at 235°F using light oak wood for smoke flavor.

Put the roast in the cooker for 3 to 4 hours, until the internal temperature reaches 125°F (for medium-rare).

Transfer the roast to a platter and tent loosely with foil. Let rest for 25 minutes. Slice it thickly or thinly to serve.

1 USDA Choice boneless rib eye roast (5 to 6 pounds)

2 tablespoons Worcestershire sauce

Chicago Ray's Prime Rib Rub (page 32)

SMOKY SKIRT STEAK FAJITAS

MAKES
10
SERVINGS

Skirt steak cooks up very nicely in the barbecue pit for these tasty fajitas. Just be sure to sharpen your knife and slice the meat thinly and always against the grain. The fajita rub and the oak smoke flavor work well together on the meat, and cooking the vegetables in the smoker puts this one over the top. This is a great way to get started with your smoker and it's a can't-miss meal.

Cut the steak into six pieces. With a heavy meat mallet, pound the steak well to tenderize it. Squeeze the juice of one lime over one side of the meat. Season with the fajita rub. (If you season it heavily, the meat will be very rich and spicy. If you like it a little milder, then season lightly.) Let rest for 5 minutes. Flip the steaks and squeeze the juice of the second lime over them. Season with the fajita rub. Place the steaks on a plate, cover with plastic wrap, and refrigerate for up to 2 hours.

Prepare your cooker to cook indirectly at 235°F using medium oak wood for smoke flavor.

continued

2 pounds USDA Choice skirt steak

2 limes

Dr. BBQ's Fired-Up Fajita Rub (page 34)

1 large red onion, halved and sliced

1 green bell pepper, halved and sliced

1 red bell pepper, halved and sliced

1 yellow bell pepper, halved and sliced

1 jalapeño, finely chopped (remove the seeds if you don't like a little heat)

¼ cup olive oil

2 teaspoons kosher salt

10 eight-inch flour tortillas

Sour cream and salsa, as needed

In a medium aluminum foil pan, combine the onion, bell peppers, and jalapeño. Drizzle with the olive oil. Season with the salt and I tablespoon of the fajita rub. Toss to mix well. Put the pan in the cooker and cook for I hour.

Wrap the tortillas tightly in aluminum foil and set aside. After the onion-pepper mixture cooks for I hour, toss it well with tongs, and then add the steak to the cooker in a single layer. Cook for 30 minutes. Toss the onion-pepper mixture and flip the steaks. Put the tortilla package in the cooker. Cook for 30 minutes.

Remove the onion-pepper mixture, tortillas, and steaks from the cooker. Tent the steaks loosely with foil and let rest for 5 minutes. Slice the steaks thinly against the grain and add to the pan with the onion-pepper mixture. Toss well and serve with the warm tortillas, sour cream, and salsa.

BIG BACON AND BLUE CHEESE–STUFFED HAMBURGERS

MAKES 4 TO 8 SERVINGS

These great big burgers have all the good stuff on the inside. They're stuffed with blue cheese and bacon and cooked in the smoker for an extra layer of flavor. Be sure to get them sealed up tight so the good stuff stays inside. They're so big you might want to serve some of them whole and some cut in half. This will keep the lighter eaters happy and make for a nice presentation.

Prepare your cooker to cook indirectly at 235°F using medium pecan wood for smoke flavor.

Divide the ground beef into eight equal portions. Flatten each portion into a thin patty about 4 inches across. On top of four of the patties, put ¼ cup of the blue cheese. Top with one quarter of the bacon and then another ground beef patty. Crimp the edges together and shape the burgers, making sure the edges are sealed.

2 pounds ground chuck

1 cup crumbled blue cheese

6 slices bacon, cooked and crumbled

Barbecue Rub #67 (page 29)

4 onion rolls, split

4 slices tomato

continued

Season the burgers liberally on both sides with the rub. Place them in the cooker for I hour. Flip and cook for about another I hour, until the beef reaches an internal temperature of I55°F.

Transfer the burgers to a plate and tent them loosely with foil. Let rest for 5 minutes. Place the burgers on the roll bottoms. Top each with a slice of tomato and the top of the bun. Serve whole or cut the sandwiches in half for smaller servings.

MEAT LOAF WITH DR PEPPER BARBECUE SAUCE

2 tablespoons olive oil

1 small onion, finely chopped

1 small green bell pepper, finely chopped

1 garlic clove, crushed

2 pounds ground chuck

2 eggs

Dr Pepper Barbecue sauce (page 42)

2 teaspoons Barbecue Rub #67 (page 29), plus additional for seasoning

1 teaspoon soy sauce

1 teaspoon salt

1 teaspoon black pepper

½ cup panko bread crumbs

Meat loaf from the barbecue pit is simple but never boring, and your family will love it—especially when it's full of onions, garlic, bell peppers, and Dr Pepper Barbecue Sauce, like this one. You cook it in a loaf pan until it sets up, then finish it right on the grill where it can pick up that great smoker flavor.

Prepare your cooker to cook indirectly at 235°F using medium pecan wood for smoke flavor.

Heat the olive oil in a medium skillet over medium heat. Add the onion, bell pepper, and garlic and cook, stirring often for 5 minutes, until the onion is soft. Transfer the vegetables to a plate and refrigerate for 10 minutes to cool.

In a big bowl, crumble the ground chuck. Add the eggs, ¼ cup of the barbecue sauce, the rub, soy sauce, salt, pepper, and the cooled onion mixture. Mix very well with your hands. Add the bread crumbs and mix well. Transfer the meat loaf mixture to a 9-by-5-inch loaf pan, pushing down to get rid of any air pockets. Place the loaf in the cooker and cook for 45 minutes. Turn the loaf out of the pan onto the cooking grate. If your cooking grates are widely spaced, you may need to use a grill topper (see page 22). Season the top liberally with more of the rub and continue cooking until the internal temperature reaches 155°F, about another 1½ hours.

Transfer the meat loaf to a plate and tent it loosely with foil. Let rest for 15 minutes. Slice and serve with extra barbecue sauce on the side.

THE BIRDS

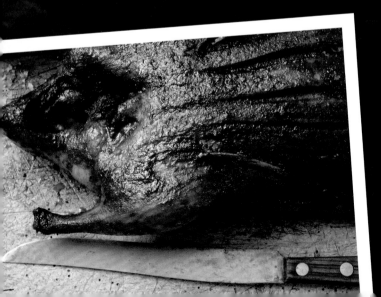

Chicken is sort of the red-headed stepchild of the barbecue world. No particular barbecue region or style really wants to claim it as their own, but they all seem to like it. Chicken is sort of taken for granted. It's just always there. Just about any barbecue joint will serve you a half-chicken dinner or a pulled-chicken sandwich, and surely a lot of people are eating and enjoying it. But you never hear about a group of guys driving across the country sampling barbecued chicken as they go. Those stories are reserved for the more noble pigs and cows of the culinary world. But chicken is often called upon for the big barbecue at the VFW or American Legion events because it cooks pretty quickly, it's economical, and everybody likes it.

To cook great chicken at home, you have to start by reading the label. Much of the chicken at the supermarket has been "enhanced," which is a nice word for saying it has been pumped with a salt water mixture. It's similar to a brine, but usually also contains phosphates and some flavoring agents. What this all does is keep the chicken fresh longer and it allows the home cook to overcook it a little without drying it out. This really isn't a terrible thing and most of us regularly eat this chicken without even knowing it. But not all enhanced chicken is created equal. Some of it is much better than others because of the flavoring of choice, the amount of salt, and the amount of phosphates. If you read the label and pay attention to how you like the different brands, you may find one that you really like. You may also find that you don't like any

of them and that you prefer chicken that hasn't been enhanced. If you check around, you'll probably find a local supermarket that sells non-enhanced chicken at a fair price. The label for this should say "all natural" and have no mention of enhancement. You may also want to try organic chicken. Many cooks prefer this as a chicken that tastes more like chicken. The price will be a little higher and the chickens may be a little smaller, but it's generally pretty good stuff. The best suggestion I can make is to find the chicken brand that you like and stick with it. It's the only way to perfect your cooking techniques and to be able to get it done right consistently.

> . . . chicken is often called upon for the big barbecue . . . because it cooks pretty quickly, it's economical, and everybody likes it.

Turkeys are a similar story, except it can be hard to find one that hasn't been enhanced without visiting a specialty shop and paying a premium. It can also be hard to find one when it's not Thanksgiving or Christmas. As for ducks and Cornish hens, where I live there's pretty much one choice in the freezer case but they're usually pretty good. If you live where you have several choices, I envy you. Pick a good one and enjoy.

The main reason for all of this enhancing of birds is that we tend to overcook them and then they get dry and nobody likes a dry piece of meat. Like so many things that we cook, poultry is best when cooked to the correct degree of doneness. The proper temperatures for juicy cooked poultry are 160°F in the breast and 180°F in the thigh. This isn't always possible, though, when cooking whole or half birds, so the enhancement can be your friend. But if you're cooking non-enhanced birds, there are some easy tricks to help.

You inject the marinade deeply into the meat where it helps keep things juicy and makes it taste great.

The oldest trick in the book is brining. You dissolve 1 cup of salt in 1 gallon of water and you have a basic brine. Add 1 cup of sugar and some flavors and you have a really good brine. Without getting too far into the science, brining transfers the salty water into the meat along with the flavors and it stays in while you cook the meat. This makes it all a little more forgiving if you overcook things a little and it makes the bird taste good throughout. The other option is to inject the bird with a marinade. Soaking in a marinade just doesn't work very well, but those little injectors in the kitchen department work great. You inject the marinade deeply into the meat where it helps keep things juicy and makes it taste great.

The basic cooking plan for chicken in the smoker is to season it with a brine, marinade, or dry rub. Then cook it until it reaches an internal temperature of 160°F for white meat and 180°F for dark meat. You'll notice the cooking temperatures are a little higher for poultry. That's because it's a tender and smaller piece of meat that doesn't need that long slow cooking. The higher temp will also keep the skin from getting rubbery, a common problem with slow-cooked birds. You can use a whole bird or any of the parts and you can tweak the taste in a lot of ways because chicken goes well with many flavors. If we all keep cooking great chicken, maybe someday it will have its own home!

OLD-SCHOOL BARBECUED CHICKEN

MAKES
2 TO 4
SERVINGS

This is the genesis of all barbecued chicken and something everybody loves. We've all been served a barbecued half-chicken dinner at a local fundraiser and with the friendly atmosphere and a good cause it makes for a pretty good meal. But a little brine and some homemade barbecue sauce will make your chicken barbecue something very special and your friends will all be asking you to make it again.

To make the brine: Heat I cup water in a small saucepan over medium heat until it's about to simmer. Add the salt, sugar, onion powder, garlic powder, and pepper. Mix well and cook until the salt and sugar have dissolved, about 4 minutes. Transfer to a bowl or small pitcher and mix in the ice water. Refrigerate until very cold.

Put the chicken halves in a gallon-size plastic zip bag. Pour the brine over them. Squeeze out as much air as possible and seal the bag. Refrigerate for 3 hours, turning occasionally.

continued

BRINE

2 tablespoons kosher salt

1 tablespoon sugar

1 teaspoon onion powder

1 teaspoon garlic powder

1 teaspoon black pepper

1 cup ice water

1 frying chicken (4 to 5 pounds), cut in half

Barbecue Rub #67 (page 29)

Thick and Rich Barbecue Sauce (page 38)

Prepare your cooker to cook indirectly at 250°F using medium cherry wood for smoke flavor.

Take the chicken out of the bag and rinse well. Dry thoroughly and sprinkle it lightly with the rub. Put the chicken in the cooker and cook for 3 hours. Brush it with the barbecue sauce and continue cooking until each half reaches an internal temperature of 160°F in the breast and 180°F in the thigh, about another 1 hour.

Transfer the chicken to a platter and tent loosely with foil. Let rest for 10 minutes. Serve the chicken halves with additional sauce on the side.

CHICKEN ON A THRONE

MAKES
2 TO **4**
SERVINGS

½ cup butter, at room temperature

2 garlic cloves, crushed

3 tablespoons Superchicken Wing Rub (page 35)

1 frying chicken (4 to 5 pounds)

1 lemon, cut into thin wedges

½ onion, sliced thinly

One 12-ounce can beer

This is the classic chicken cooked on a beer can with a little twist. The use of a cake pan and an open Christmas tree–style stand for the chicken create a better steaming/flavoring effect in and around it. This is a great way to smoke chicken for use in tacos and casseroles as well. If you don't have a stand available, just punch in the top of the beer can, put the lemon and onion in the can, and place the chicken on the can.

Prepare your cooker to cook indirectly at 250°F using medium cherry wood for smoke flavor.

In a small bowl, mix together the butter, garlic, and 1 tablespoon of the rub. Pushing your fingers under the chicken's skin, loosen it from the meat of the breasts, thighs, and legs, being careful not to tear it. Spread the butter mixture all over the meat under the skin. Then massage the outside of the skin with the butter that's on your hands, coating it evenly all over. Season the outside and the cavity with the remaining 2 tablespoons rub.

Place the lemon and onion in a round cake pan that will fit underneath the chicken stand. Put the pan in the cooker. Pour the beer over the lemon and onion. Place the chicken on the stand and place the stand in the pan. Cook until the internal temperature of the breast meat reaches 160°F and the thigh meat reaches 180°F, about 5 to 6 hours.

Transfer the chicken on the stand to a clean pan. Tent loosely with foil and let rest for 10 minutes. Carefully remove the chicken from the stand and cut it into quarters to serve.

SUPERCHICKEN SMOKED WINGS

MAKES
12
SERVINGS

Chicken wings and spicy barbecue sauce are a great combination, and when you add the great smoke flavor from the barbecue pit, they're even better. They're an inexpensive and simple way to get started smoking, too. This recipe calls for a fairly tame hot sauce, but for those of you who dare, feel free to fire it up with a habanero or even a ghost pepper hot sauce.

Prepare your cooker to cook indirectly at 250°F using light cherry wood for smoke flavor.

In a small bowl, mix together the barbecue sauce and hot sauce. Set aside.

Cut the tips off the wings and discard. Slash each wing in the joint, just through the skin but leaving the wing intact. Season the wings liberally on all sides with the rub. Put them in the cooker and cook for 2 hours. Brush the wings with the sauce mixture, then flip and brush the other sides. Continue cooking, brushing and flipping every 30 minutes, for another 1½ hours, or until the wings are very tender.

Transfer the wings to a platter and tent loosely with foil. Let rest for 5 minutes. Serve the wings hot with extra hot sauce, if desired.

½ cup Thin and Spicy Barbecue Sauce (page 39)

½ cup Louisiana hot sauce, plus more for serving (optional)

12 whole fresh chicken wings

Superchicken Wing Rub (page 35)

COMPETITION-STYLE BARBECUED CHICKEN THIGHS

BRINE

2 tablespoons kosher salt

2 tablespoons brown sugar

½ teaspoon onion powder

½ teaspoon garlic powder

¼ teaspoon cayenne pepper

8 chicken thighs with only the leg bone

Ray's Supersweet Rib Rub (page 31)

½ cup margarine

1 cup Thick and Rich Barbecue Sauce (page 38)

¼ cup honey

The big-time cook-off guys do some very strange things to try to win, but their chicken is about the strangest. This isn't what most people cook at home, but this type of turn-in wins most of the big barbecue contests around the country. There is really no explanation except that in blind judging, it almost always gets a good score. At home it tastes pretty good too, just a little different from what you'd expect.

To make the brine: The night before you plan to cook, combine 2 cups water with the salt, brown sugar, onion powder, garlic powder, and cayenne in a small saucepan over medium-high heat. Bring to a simmer, stirring often. Cook for 3 to 4 minutes, until the salt and sugar have dissolved. Transfer to a small pitcher or bowl to cool. Refrigerate for at least 4 hours, until very cold.

Trim the meat of the thighs to make them rectangular and all the same size, retaining as much skin as possible. Four hours before you plan to cook, place the chicken thighs in a plastic zip bag and pour the brine over them. Press out all the air and seal the bag. Refrigerate, turning the bag occasionally, for 3 hours.

Remove the chicken from the brine and dry well with a paper towel. Place the chicken on a rack to dry further. Refrigerate for 30 minutes.

Prepare your cooker to cook indirectly at 250°F using light cherry wood for smoke flavor.

Season the chicken liberally with the rub. Tuck the skin under the thighs and return the thighs to the rack at room temperature for 20 minutes. Put the chicken in the cooker, skin-side up, for 30 minutes. Melt the margarine in an aluminum foil pan big enough to hold the chicken in a single layer. Transfer the chicken to the pan, turning to coat and placing it skin-side up. Cover the pan tightly with aluminum foil. Return it to the cooker until the chicken reaches an internal temperature of 190°F, about 1 hour.

In a small bowl, mix together the barbecue sauce and honey. Take the chicken out of the pan and return it to the cooker, skin-side up. Brush the thighs with sauce on the top and bottom, being careful not to damage the skin. Cook for 20 minutes.

Transfer the thighs to a platter and tent loosely with foil. Let rest for 5 minutes before serving.

LEMON AND HERB– SMOKED CHICKEN LEGS

MAKES
10
SERVINGS

⅓ cup olive oil

1 lemon, zested and juiced

4 garlic cloves, crushed

1 teaspoon dried thyme

1 teaspoon salt

½ teaspoon black pepper

10 chicken drumsticks

The classic flavor combination of citrus and herbs on chicken rises to new heights when the magic of the barbecue pit is added. The meaty, juicy legs are perfect for slow cooking and the mild apple smoke pairs beautifully with the flavors of the lemon and thyme for this white-napkin barbecue dish.

In a small bowl, combine the olive oil, lemon zest and juice, garlic, thyme, salt, and pepper. Mix well.

Place the chicken drumsticks in a large plastic zip bag. Pour the oil mixture over the legs. Press out as much air as possible and seal the bag. Refrigerate for at least 1 hour and up to 4 hours.

Prepare your cooker to cook indirectly at 250°F using mild apple wood for smoke flavor.

Remove the legs from the bag and place them on the cooking grid. Cook until the internal temperature of the legs reaches 180°F, about 1½ hours.

Transfer the chicken to a plate and tent loosely with foil. Let rest for 5 minutes before serving.

STATE FAIR TURKEY LEGS

Everybody loves those big smoked turkey legs that we get at the fair to carry around, eating like a caveman. With this simple recipe, you can make them at home and enjoy them all the time. The secret to their goodness is in the brine. It keeps them moist and juicy and makes them taste great.

To make the brine: Heat I cup water in a small saucepan over medium heat until it's about to simmer. Add the salt, sugar, pepper, chipotle, sage, and onion powder. Mix well and cook until the salt and sugar have dissolved, about 4 minutes. Transfer to a bowl or small pitcher and mix in the ice water. Refrigerate until very cold.

Put the turkey legs in a gallon-size plastic zip bag. Pour the brine over them. Squeeze out as much air as possible and seal the bag. Refrigerate for 3 hours, turning occasionally.

Prepare your cooker to cook indirectly at 250°F using medium cherry wood for smoke flavor.

Remove the legs from the bag and rinse well. Dry thoroughly and sprinkle lightly with the rub. Put the legs in the cooker and cook for 3 hours. Brush with the barbecue sauce and continue cooking until they reach an internal temperature of 180°F, about another I hour.

Transfer the legs to a platter and tent loosely with foil. Let rest for 5 minutes before serving.

BRINE

2 tablespoons kosher salt

1 tablespoon sugar

1 teaspoon black pepper

1 teaspoon ground chipotle

1 teaspoon rubbed sage

1 teaspoon onion powder

1 cup ice water

4 turkey legs (about 3 pounds total)

Barbecue Rub #67 (page 29)

Thick and Rich Barbecue Sauce (page 38)

SCOTTIE'S CREOLE BUTTER

2 cups butter

One 12-ounce can beer

1 tablespoon barbecue rub of your choice

1 tablespoon paprika

1 tablespoon white pepper

1 tablespoon finely ground black pepper

1 tablespoon sea salt

1 tablespoon garlic powder

1 tablespoon onion powder

1 tablespoon dry mustard powder

1 teaspoon cayenne pepper

1 turkey (about 15 pounds), fully defrosted

Barbecue Rub #68 (page 30)

1 onion, quartered

1 apple, quartered

Ice cubes

LOUISIANA-STYLE THANKSGIVING TURKEY

MAKES
12
SERVINGS

The Creole butter that's used in this recipe comes from my friend Scottie Johnson, and it's a good one. Injecting the turkey with butter gives it a great flavor deep inside and helps keep it moist and juicy. Scottie is a fantastic barbecue cook who won the Jack Daniel's World Barbecue Championship in 2006. Scottie and his beautiful daughters, Zoe and Lexi, run CancerSucksChicago.com in memory of their mom, Corliss, who left us way too early.

To make the Creole butter: Melt the butter in a small saucepan. Add the beer, rub, paprika, both peppers, salt, garlic powder, onion powder, dry mustard, and cayenne. Mix well and remove from the heat when well blended.

Tuck the wing tips behind the turkey's neck. Cover the turkey loosely with plastic wrap. Using a kitchen injector, inject small amounts of the Creole butter deeply into the turkey in a grid pattern about 1 inch apart. Continue until all the butter is gone.

Season the turkey liberally with the rub. Stuff the onion and apple into the cavity. Fill a gallon-size plastic zip bag with ice cubes and lay the bag on the breast of the turkey. This will help keep the breast meat cold until cooking time and will result in the white and dark meat getting done at the same time. Let rest at room temp for I hour.

Prepare your cooker to cook indirectly at 250°F using medium apple wood for smoke flavor.

Remove the ice pack and put the turkey in the cooker. Cook until the breast meat deep down by the wing joint reaches an internal temperature of I55°F and the thigh meat deep down by the leg joint reaches I75°F, about 5 hours.

Transfer the turkey to a platter and tent loosely with foil. Let rest for 20 minutes. The temperature will continue to rise during the rest, ensuring a fully and evenly cooked turkey throughout. Carve to serve.

BUFFALO TURKEY WINGS

2 whole fresh turkey wings

Barbecue Rub #67 (page 29)

½ cup butter, melted

½ cup Louisiana hot sauce

Turkey wings are really good cooked in the smoker and we really should cook them more often. They're kind of like giant chicken wings with a more interesting flavor. I like them with just a dry rub or glazed with traditional barbecue sauce, but this spicy buffalo version is about as good as it gets.

Prepare your cooker to cook indirectly at 235°F using medium apple wood for smoke flavor.

Cut the tips off the wings and reserve them for making stock. Slash the wings on the inside of the joint, cutting just the skin. Season the wings liberally with the rub. Put them in the cooker for 2 hours. Flip the wings and cook for 1 hour more. Transfer the wings to a foil pan and pour the butter and hot sauce over them. Toss to coat. Cover the pan with foil and return to the cooker. Cook for about 1 hour, or until very tender, tossing the wings to coat every 20 minutes.

Transfer the wings to a cutting board and separate them at the joints. Transfer them to a platter and pour the pan juices over them. Tent loosely with foil and let rest for 5 minutes before serving.

COZY CORNER-STYLE CORNISH HENS

MAKES
4
SERVINGS

Memphis is famous for the barbecued ribs and pork shoulders served all over town, and the Cozy Corner serves those with the best of them. But they also serve a barbecued Cornish hen that's even better than the ribs and pork shoulder. I'm not sure what they do to theirs, but I like to brine mine for a short time to keep them juicy and tasty throughout. This is a great dish for a party. It looks fancy, but it's easy for the new barbecue cook.

To make the brine: Heat 2 cups water in a small saucepan over medium heat. Add the lemon juice, soy sauce, honey, thyme, and pepper. Mix well and cook until the salt and honey have dissolved, about 4 minutes. Transfer to a bowl or small pitcher and mix in the ice water. Refrigerate until very cold.

Place the hens in a large plastic zip bag. Pour the brine over them. Squeeze out as much air as possible and seal the bag. Refrigerate for 3 hours, turning occasionally.

continued

BRINE

2 lemons, juiced

¼ cup soy sauce

2 tablespoons honey

1½ teaspoons dried thyme

1 teaspoon black pepper

2½ cups ice water

4 Cornish hens

Barbecue Rub #68 (page 30)

Barbecue sauce

Prepare your cooker to cook indirectly at 250°F using medium cherry wood for smoke flavor.

Take the hens out of the bag and rinse well. Dry them thoroughly and sprinkle lightly with the rub. Put the hens in the cooker, breast-side up, and cook for I hour. Flip the hens breast-side down and cook for I hour. Flip again and cook for another I hour, or until the internal temperature deep in the thigh reaches 180°F.

Transfer the hens to a platter and tent loosely with foil. Let rest for 5 minutes. Serve with barbecue sauce on the side.

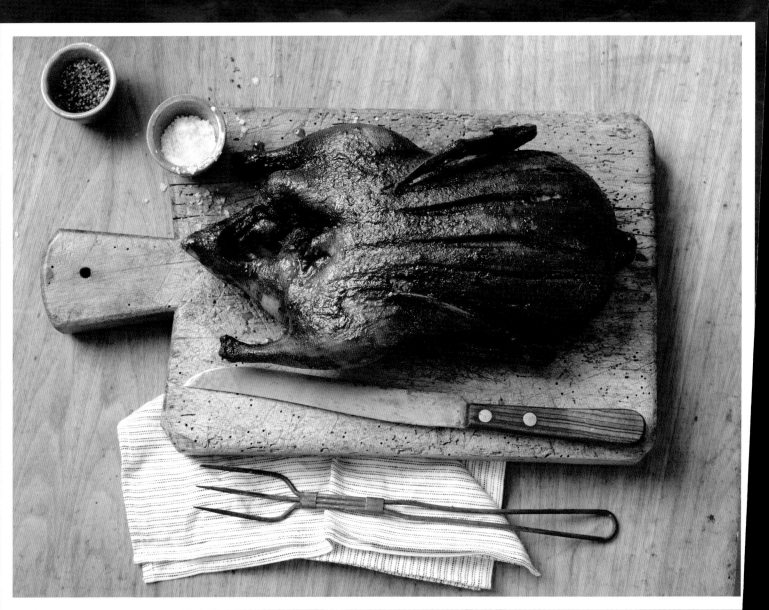

BARBECUED DUCK WITH SPICY ORANGE GLAZE

MAKES
4
SERVINGS

Duck is a great meat for the smoker because it has plenty of fat to keep things moist and juicy during the long smoking process. The meat has a big flavor that stands up well to the smoke and spicy glaze. We score the skin so the fat will render and the flavor from the glaze and smoke will work their way in. This dish is a little bit complicated, but if you can keep the smoker temperature even it will come out beautifully.

Prepare your cooker to cook indirectly at 250°F using medium pecan wood for smoke flavor.

With a small, sharp knife, score the skin along the duck breast from front to back, about ½ inch apart, cutting through the skin but not all the way to the meat. Salt the duck liberally. Then season lightly with the rub. Put the duck in the cooker, breast-side up, and cook for 2 hours. Flip the duck and cook for 1 hour more. Brush the duck all over with the barbecue sauce and flip it to the breast-up position. Continue cooking, basting every hour with the barbecue sauce, until the internal temperature deep in the thigh reaches 180°F, about another 2 hours.

Transfer the duck to a platter and tent loosely with foil. Let rest for 15 minutes. Cut the duck into quarters to serve.

1 duck (about 6 pounds), fully defrosted

Kosher salt

Barbecue Rub #68 (page 30)

Orange-Chipotle Barbecue Sauce (page 41)

CHAPTER
6

In the world of barbecue cook-offs, there are usually three to five main categories to be judged. And they're the classic barbecue dishes of chicken, ribs, pork shoulder, beef brisket, and sometimes whole hog. These meats are the cornerstone of real barbecue and the pitmasters spend many days and nights cooking and perfecting them. But cooking only those few things gets a little boring even for a barbecue man, so sometimes there's an extra category and the tradition is to call it Anything But—as in "anything but the regular categories of the day." This is a chance for the cooks to show their chops, so to speak, in areas that are not typical barbecue fare. It's also a great chance for the local contest organizers to feature something that's produced locally or even just something they think the judges would like to eat. Oh yeah, the judges really enjoy a little change of pace with the Anything But category!

Over the years, I've seen unique featured items such as turkey, cabbage, grits, chili, and dessert. But more often than not, it's an open category where the cook can choose what he wants to cook and the entries run the gamut. Many of the contests have outlawed desserts in the open category, though, because it's really not fair to judge a piece of grilled catfish against a piece of cherry cheesecake. The desserts were winning all the time! Even without desserts, it's interesting to see the variety of dishes that come to the table. The non-barbecue cooking skills of the contestants are amazing. Most of them aren't professional chefs, but they sure do know how to cook!

So I use the Anything But name for the chapter that catches all the dishes that don't quite fit anywhere else. I, too, have omitted desserts here; they are with the side dishes. You will find some wonderful non-traditional barbecue dishes—sausage, fish, shrimp, and even a smoked Scotch egg recipe. Some of these are shorter to cook, so it's fun to start them early and serve them as a treat to enjoy while the real long-cooked barbecue keeps chugging along.

SMOKED STUFFED BABY BELLAS

MAKES ABOUT
4
SERVINGS

Cremini mushrooms, also known as baby bellas, look similar to regular old button mushrooms but they pack a lot more flavor. They hold up well to cooking in the barbecue pit and to big flavors like bacon and blue cheese. These are easy to assemble and a great short-cook appetizer to enjoy while waiting for the main course to finish up.

Prepare your cooker to cook indirectly at 235°F using light apple wood for smoke flavor.

In a small bowl, mix together the blue cheese, bacon, garlic, bread crumbs, and pepper. Twist the stems out of the mushrooms and scrape out the gills, being careful not to break the sides of the mushroom caps. Place the mushroom caps on a grill topper with the bottoms facing up. Spoon the blue cheese mixture into them. Put the stuffed mushrooms in the cooker and cook for I hour, or until the mushrooms are tender.

Serve hot.

⅓ cup crumbled blue cheese

2 slices bacon, cooked and finely chopped

2 garlic cloves, crushed

1 tablespoon panko bread crumbs

¼ teaspoon black pepper

1 pound baby bella mushrooms

JAMBALAYA

3 tablespoons vegetable oil

1 red onion, chopped

1 green bell pepper, chopped

1 jalapeño, minced (remove the seeds if you don't like it hot)

3 garlic cloves, minced

2 cups (about 1 pound) chopped andouille sausage or smoked sausage

One 14½-ounce can diced tomatoes

1 tablespoon paprika

2 teaspoons dried thyme

2 teaspoons kosher salt

½ teaspoon black pepper

¼ teaspoon cayenne pepper

3 cups chicken broth, plus more if needed

2 cups chopped, cooked chicken (smoked or roasted)

1 cup uncooked white rice

4 large red bell peppers

4 large green bell peppers

JAMBALAYA-STUFFED BELL PEPPERS

Instead of plain old rice stuffing, we're kicking it up a notch here with some great Louisiana flavors, as these bell peppers get a new twist with jambalaya for a stuffing. The spicy andouille sausage really makes a difference, so try to find it if you can. Add an extra jalapeño if you dare and mix the colors of the bell peppers for a great presentation.

To make the jambalaya: In a Dutch oven over medium heat, warm the vegetable oil. Add the onion and chopped bell pepper and cook for 4 minutes, stirring often. Add the jalapeño and garlic and cook for 4 minutes, stirring often. Add the sausage and cook for 4 minutes, stirring often. Add the tomatoes, paprika, thyme, salt, pepper, and cayenne. Mix well and cook for 4 minutes, stirring often. Add the broth and chicken and bring to a simmer, stirring occasionally. Add the rice and mix well. Return to a simmer. Cover and cook, stirring occasionally, for about 20 minutes, or until

continued

the rice is soft and most of the liquid is absorbed. If the liquid evaporates too quickly, add some additional chicken broth. Remove from the heat and let rest for 10 minutes.

Prepare your cooker to cook indirectly at 235°F using medium pecan wood for smoke flavor.

Cut the tops off the red and green bell peppers and remove the veins and seeds. Cut a little off the bottom if needed to get the peppers to stand up, but be careful not to cut all the way through. Stuff the peppers with the jambalaya and stand them up on a grill topper. Put the peppers in the cooker for 1½ hours, or until the peppers are tender.

Remove from the cooker and transfer the peppers to a platter. Tent loosely with foil and let rest for 5 minutes before serving.

SMOKED SCOTCH EGGS

MAKES

12

SERVINGS

Sausage-wrapped "Scotch" eggs are a tasty and interesting dish when breaded and fried in the traditional manner, but cooking them on the smoker makes a very special treat. The homemade sausage gets a nice crust on the outside and, if you get it cooked just right, the egg yolk will have a little bit of ooze on the inside. Just make sure to seal the sausage all the way around the egg before smoking. I like to serve these as an appetizer, but they are also fine as a nice smoked addition to a lunch salad.

Put the eggs in a medium saucepan and cover with cold water. Let rest for 15 minutes to warm them up before cooking. (This will help keep them from cracking.) Over high heat, bring the eggs to a boil, rolling them around in the pot frequently. When the water begins to boil, start timing and cook for 2 minutes, continuing to roll the eggs around in the pan. (This will keep the yolks in the center.) Remove the eggs

6 large eggs

Ice water

1 pound ground pork

1 teaspoon salt

1 teaspoon black pepper

1 teaspoon garlic powder

¼ teaspoon cayenne pepper

Barbecue Rub #67 (page 29)

Barbecue sauce

continued

from the boiling water quickly and submerge them in ice water to stop the cooking. When the eggs are cool, peel them and refrigerate.

Put the pork in a medium bowl and add the salt, pepper, garlic powder, and cayenne. Mix well and then divide the sausage into six equal portions. On waxed paper, flatten out one of the portions to a 4-inch circle. Top with an egg and wrap the sausage all around the egg, stretching as needed and sealing it completely. Do this with all the eggs and then season them liberally with the rub. Put the eggs on a pan lined with waxed paper and refrigerate for 1 hour.

Prepare your cooker to cook indirectly at 235°F using medium pecan wood for smoke flavor.

Place the eggs on a grill topper or directly on the cooking grate and cook for 1 hour and 15 minutes, or until golden brown and firm to the touch.

Transfer the eggs to a plate and let cool. Cut them in halves or quarters and serve with barbecue sauce for dipping.

¼ cup ice water

3 garlic cloves, crushed

1 tablespoon kosher salt

1 tablespoon paprika

1 teaspoon black pepper

1 teaspoon sugar

1 teaspoon dried marjoram

1 pound ground chuck

1 pound ground pork

BIG-TIME KIELBASA ROLL

Smoking sausage to preserve it is a long-standing barbecue tradition, but these days we usually just do it to make the sausage taste good. Homemade sausage is really just ground meat mixed with some spices, and it's simple to do at home. The Internet has created a popular fad of smoking a "fatty," which is really just a big sausage roll without casing. Here is my Chicago-style kielbasa-inspired version of a fatty. Serve with crackers, raw onion, and Yellow Barbecue Sauce (page 40).

Prepare your cooker to cook indirectly at 235°F using medium apple wood for smoke flavor.

In a small bowl, combine the ice water, garlic, salt, paprika, pepper, sugar, and marjoram. Mix well and set aside.

In a large bowl, mix together the ground chuck and the ground pork. Top with the spice mixture and mix well with your hands until well blended. Lay out a sheet of aluminum foil about 12 inches by 16 inches. Form the kielbasa into a uniform log about 10 inches long and lay it on the foil. Roll the log up in the foil, sealing both ends like a candy wrapper. Put the kielbasa directly on the cooking grate and cook for 30 minutes. Open the foil, leaving the kielbasa on it, and roll the kielbasa over so the flat side is on top. Cook for another 30 minutes. The kielbasa should now be firmed up and round. Remove it from the foil completely and transfer the kielbasa directly to the cooking grate. Cook until the internal temperature reaches 165°F, about 2 hours longer.

Transfer the sausage to a platter and tent loosely with foil. Let rest for 10 minutes. Slice to serve.

BARBECUED BOLOGNA

One 3-pound chub or chunk bologna

Barbecue Rub #68 (page 30)

Bologna is a popular smoked meat in the South and it's quite good. You'll need to start with a big chunk though; sliced deli bologna just won't work. The cooking process firms it up, gives it a great smoky flavor, and develops a little crust on the outside. It's delicious served at room temperature with crackers and cheese or on white bread with barbecue sauce and thinly sliced onion for a tasty sandwich.

Prepare your cooker to cook indirectly at 235°F using medium cherry wood for smoke flavor.

Slice off a thin piece off the bologna lengthwise so it has a flat bottom and won't roll around. Score the top in a series of thin slashes in a diamond pattern. Season the bologna liberally with the rub. Put the bologna in the cooker and cook for at least 3 hours but up to 5 hours. It's already fully cooked, so the recipe is very flexible, but as it cooks longer it will get smokier and develop a better outside crust.

Transfer the bologna to a cutting board. Tent loosely with foil and let rest for 5 minutes. Slice to serve.

HERBY RUBBED LEG OF LAMB

1 boneless lamb leg, rolled (4 to 5 pounds)

2 garlic cloves, cut into slivers

2 tablespoons olive oil

Herby Rub (page 36)

Leg of lamb has a big, bold flavor that holds up very well to cooking in the barbecue pit. The traditional garlic and herb seasonings take on a whole new flavor profile when a little smoke is added to the mix. Try serving it with traditional barbecue side dishes and barbecue sauce on the side for dipping. This is a nice way to smoke your holiday dinner.

Prepare your cooker to cook indirectly at 235°F using medium grapevine or wine-barrel wood for smoke flavor.

With a long, narrow knife, pierce the lamb deeply in a few spots on all sides. Push the garlic deeply into the holes. Rub the olive oil all over the lamb. Season the lamb liberally with the rub on all sides. Let rest at room temperature for 20 minutes.

Put the lamb in the cooker, fat-side up. Cook for about 3 hours, until it reaches an internal temperature of 150°F for medium-rare.

Transfer the lamb to a platter and tent loosely with foil. Let rest for 20 minutes. Slice thinly to serve.

CREAMY SMOKED TILAPIA SPREAD

MAKES

6

SERVINGS

The mild flavor of tilapia gets kicked up with a little smoke for this recipe. Then it gets paired with some great ingredients to make a Florida favorite—smoked fish spread. Try serving this with a variety of crackers, hot sauce, and thinly sliced raw onions on the side. I cook the fish to a well-done state. This is best done the day before you plan to make the spread, then the spread itself can be made a few hours before serving.

Prepare your cooker to cook indirectly at 235°F using medium pecan wood for smoke flavor.

Cut the fillets in half and season lightly with the rub. Cook for 1½ hours, or until very firm. Transfer to a plate to cool. Cover and refrigerate until chilled.

In a large bowl, break the tilapia into small pieces and set aside.

In a medium bowl, combine the cream cheese, mayonnaise, most of the green onions (reserving some tops for garnish), the hot sauce, lemon zest, salt, and pepper. Mix well.

Pour the cream cheese over the tilapia and fold gently until combined. Cover with plastic wrap and refrigerate for at least 1 hour.

To serve, transfer the spread to a bowl and top with the reserved green onion tops for garnish.

SMOKED TILAPIA

1 pound tilapia fillets

Barbecue Rub #68 (page 30)

One 8-ounce tub whipped cream cheese

¼ cup mayonnaise

6 green onions, white and green parts sliced thinly

1 tablespoon Louisiana hot sauce

½ lemon, zested

¼ teaspoon salt

¼ teaspoon black pepper

SMOKED SALMON WITH HONEY-ORANGE GLAZE

BRINE

2 tablespoons kosher salt

1 tablespoon brown sugar

½ teaspoon onion powder

½ teaspoon black pepper

¼ teaspoon ground cinnamon

1 cup ice water

1½ to 2 pounds boneless salmon fillets

GLAZE

3 tablespoons honey

1 tablespoon freshly squeezed orange juice

1 orange, zested

⅛ teaspoon fresh thyme

Paprika

Salmon and the smoker are like peanut butter and jelly. It seems that no matter what you do, smoked salmon turns out to be a winner. It's simple to cook at home, but seems so elegant on the table. Just make sure the fish you buy is very fresh. For this recipe the salmon gets a quick brine to make it juicy and tasty on the inside, while honey and fresh orange make up a great glaze for the outside.

To make the brine: Combine 1 cup water with the salt, brown sugar, onion powder, pepper, and cinnamon in a small saucepan over medium heat. Bring to a simmer and cook for 4 minutes, stirring often until well blended. Transfer to a bowl. Add the ice water and mix well. Refrigerate until cold. The brine needs to be very cold before using.

One hour before you plan to cook, put the salmon in a heavy-duty gallon-size plastic zip bag. Pour the brine over the salmon. Push out as much air as possible and seal the bag. Refrigerate for 1 hour.

To make the glaze: Add the honey, orange juice, orange zest, and thyme to a small bowl and mix well. Set aside.

Prepare your cooker to cook indirectly at 235°F using medium alder wood for smoke flavor.

Remove the salmon from the bag and dry well with a paper towel. Dust lightly with paprika. Place the salmon skin-side down on a grill topper in the cooker. Cook the salmon for 30 minutes, or until the white fat just begins to bubble up through the fish.

Transfer the salmon to a plate and brush with the glaze. Let rest for 5 minutes. Eat warm as an entrée or chill and serve cold or at room temperature as an hors d'oeuvre.

PLANKED SALMON WITH SOY-HONEY GLAZE

MAKES
4
SERVINGS

Salmon cooked on a plank picks up just a hint of the wood flavor while it cooks, and the flavor of the sweet and salty glaze combines with it perfectly. The plank makes for a dramatic presentation when it's brought to the table, and with the salmon already cut into serving pieces, guests can serve themselves the piece that looks just right.

Soak an alder wood cooking plank in water for I hour. Prepare your cooker to cook indirectly at 250°F using light alder wood smoke for flavor.

Place the salmon pieces on the plank, spacing them evenly apart. Salt the salmon lightly and place the plank in the cooker. Cook for 30 minutes.

To make the glaze: Combine the hoisin, soy sauce, honey, sesame oil, and pepper in a small bowl. Mix well with a spoon.

After the fish has cooked for 30 minutes, spoon half of the glaze over the top, coating it evenly. Cook for another 20 minutes. Spoon the rest of the glaze over the top and cook until the fish is firm, about another 20 minutes.

Transfer the whole plank to a sheet pan and take the whole thing to the table to serve.

1½ pounds boneless, skinless salmon fillet, cut into 4 pieces

Salt

SOY-HONEY GLAZE

½ cup hoisin sauce

2 tablespoons soy sauce

2 tablespoons honey

1 teaspoon sesame oil

¼ teaspoon black pepper

SMOKED SHRIMP COCKTAIL

1 pound extra-large shrimp, peeled and deveined, tails on

Barbecue Rub #68 (page 30)

SAUCE

½ cup tomato-based barbecue sauce

¼ cup mayonnaise

1 teaspoon prepared horseradish

1 lemon, zested

A smoked shrimp cocktail is a wonderful way to start any meal, but a particularly good way to start a barbecue meal. It's easy to do and can be elegant. Try putting a little bit of the sauce in a martini glass with the shrimp hanging on the rim for that special-occasion look. This one is great for making ahead, too, to keep your guests occupied while you're working on the main course.

Prepare your cooker to cook indirectly at 235°F using light hickory wood for smoke flavor.

Season the shrimp liberally with the rub. If you're using a stovetop smoker, place the shrimp directly on the cooking grate. Otherwise, place them on a grill topper and place the grill topper in the cooker. Cook for 15 minutes, and then flip the shrimp. Cook for another 15 minutes, or until they are pink and firm to the touch.

Transfer the shrimp to a platter, cover with plastic wrap, and refrigerate.

To make the sauce: Mix the barbecue sauce, mayonnaise, horseradish, and lemon zest in a small bowl. Whisk together. Cover with plastic wrap and refrigerate.

Take the shrimp and the sauce out of the refrigerator fifteen minutes before serving.

CHAPTER

7

THE NECESSARY
SIDE DISHES

Barbecue never takes the back seat, no matter what else is being served. Fried chicken, tamales, fried turkey, catfish, and great stews like gumbo and burgoo are commonly served as a second main course, but with barbecue on the table they always play second fiddle. And while we enjoy the second fiddle, we could be almost as happy without it. Barbecue is just that important and that loved by everyone. The passion put into it by the cook is clearly reflected in the reverence of the diners. But even these obsessed fans can't live on meat alone. They need and they want great side dishes. And the choices are important.

Baked beans, often cooked in the smoker right next to the barbecue, are the all-time number-one barbecue side. If you go to a barbecue restaurant that doesn't serve beans, leave. They can be dried pinto beans or canned baked beans, and both are appreciated for their style. Next up is coleslaw. Many barbecue joints put the slaw right on top of the barbecue in their sandwiches, so it'd better be good. Creamy or tangy is fine.

Mostly that depends on where you live. Potato salad is a good choice, too. So is mac and cheese, but don't try anything fancy. The good old cheesy stuff is best. Grits are a welcome side dish with barbecue.

This is starting to sound like Southern food or even soul food, isn't it? Well, that's because it is.

This is starting to sound like Southern food or even soul food, isn't it? Well, that's because it is. Barbecue *is* Southern food and it *is* soul food. And the side dishes are a big part of both of those cuisines. So think about that when you plan your menu. No sprouts or tofu need apply. But keep in mind that even The World's Greatest Banana Pudding (page 171) plays second fiddle to great barbecue.

CAROLINA-STYLE SLAW

MAKES
4 TO 6
SERVINGS

⅓ cup olive oil

2 tablespoons cider vinegar

2 tablespoons sugar

1 teaspoon salt

¼ teaspoon black pepper

1 pound shredded coleslaw mix

Carolina slaw is definitely not a creamy mayo type. It's tart and tangy and it matches beautifully with sweet smoky barbecue, especially pork shoulder. This is a great slaw to top a barbecue sandwich with. Try serving it on the side, but suggest that the guests try it as a topping. You'll probably make some quick converts.

In a small bowl, combine the olive oil, vinegar, sugar, salt, and pepper. Mix well and set aside.

Place the coleslaw mix in a large bowl and toss to break it apart. Pour the oil mixture over the slaw mix. Toss well. Let rest for 5 minutes and toss again. Use immediately or cover with plastic wrap and refrigerate for up to 1 hour before serving.

BACON AND BLUE CHEESE COLESLAW

MAKES ABOUT
8
SERVINGS

The combination of ranch dressing, bacon, and blue cheese make this slaw a real winner and it's easy to do when you use a packaged slaw mix. See if your guests can figure out that the unique taste is ranch dressing. Or maybe just keep that as your secret. While some slaws do well as a sandwich topping, this one is best served on the side with ribs or beef brisket.

In a small bowl, whisk together the ranch dressing, sugar, maple syrup, and pepper. Set aside.

In a large bowl, add the coleslaw mix, bacon, and blue cheese. Toss to mix well. Add the dressing mix and toss to blend well.

Refrigerate for at least 30 minutes and up to I hour. Toss well and serve.

1 cup ranch dressing

1 tablespoon sugar

1 tablespoon maple syrup

¼ teaspoon black pepper

1 pound shredded coleslaw mix

4 slices bacon, cooked crispy and crumbled

½ cup crumbled blue cheese

6 slices bacon, finely diced

1 cup chopped onion

One 55-ounce can baked beans

1 cup Thick and Rich Barbecue Sauce (page 38)

⅓ cup packed dark brown sugar

¼ cup sweet spicy mustard

SANDI'S SWEET 'N' SPICY BAKED BEANS

Beans are a staple with any barbecue meal, and it seems everybody has a secret recipe. This one comes from my honey, Sandi. Her beans won a big award for our cook-off team at the American Royal Barbecue Cook-Off in Kansas City because they're really good! It's a pretty simple recipe, but when you use really good ingredients, a few is all you need.

Preheat the oven to 350°F or the smoker to 235°F.

In a medium skillet over medium heat, cook the bacon until crispy, about 10 minutes. Remove the bacon with a slotted spoon, leaving the fat in the pan. Add the onion and cook for about 5 minutes, until soft.

In a large bowl, gently mix together the beans, barbecue sauce, brown sugar, mustard, the onion, and bacon. When well blended, transfer everything to an oven-safe pan. (If you're cooking these in the smoker, an aluminum foil pan is best.)

Bake until hot and bubbly and browned on top. This will take about 1 hour in the oven or 3 hours in the smoker. Serve immediately.

JUDY'S LITTLE RED POTATO SALAD

MAKES
8
SERVINGS

Potato salad is a very common side dish for barbecue, and while it's easy to just buy it at the store, homemade is always better. There are many different kinds and most of us have a definite favorite. This version uses red potatoes with the skin on and a mayonnaise dressing. It was created by my friend Judy and I think it's a winner.

In a large kettle of salted boiling water, cook the potatoes until tender. Drain and submerge them in a large bowl of ice water. Let the potatoes cool for 5 minutes and drain.

Cut the potatoes into I-inch cubes. Put them in a large bowl. Top with the mayonnaise, onion, celery, relish, mustard, pimiento, salt, and pepper. Toss gently with a large spoon until well blended. Cover with plastic wrap and refrigerate for at least 30 minutes and up to I day.

Mix well and garnish with paprika before serving.

3 pounds small red potatoes

Ice water

2½ cups mayonnaise

½ cup diced red onion

½ cup diced celery

2 tablespoons dill pickle relish

1 tablespoon yellow mustard

1 tablespoon chopped red pimiento

1½ teaspoons kosher salt

½ teaspoon black pepper

Paprika

TWICE-SMOKED CHEESY POTATOES

2 baking potatoes

Olive oil

Kosher salt

1 cup shredded mild Cheddar cheese

¾ cup half-and-half

15 green onions, white and green parts sliced

2 tablespoons butter

½ teaspoon salt

½ teaspoon black pepper

¼ teaspoon garlic powder

Paprika

These may seem a little fancy for a barbecue side dish, but they're really tasty, and since I'm cooking them in the smoker I think they'll be accepted. They do fine in the oven, too. Just make sure nobody is looking.

Prepare your cooker to cook indirectly at 235°F using any wood for smoke flavor.

Coat the potatoes lightly with olive oil and liberally with salt. Put them in the cooker until they are soft, about 2½ hours. Cut them in half lengthwise and let cool for 15 minutes.

Scoop out the flesh into a bowl. Add the cheese, half-and-half, green onions, butter, salt, pepper, and garlic powder. Mix well until fully blended. Put the mixture back into the potato shells and sprinkle them lightly with paprika. Place the potatoes on a grill topper for easy handling. Return to the cooker and cook for 1 hour, until they're hot and lightly browned.

Transfer the potatoes to a platter to serve.

CHEESY JALAPEÑO GRITS

MAKES ABOUT

8

SERVINGS

Grits are a true Southern thing and that's where barbecue started, so everybody enjoys having them together—especially these grown-up kind of grits. These are a little cheesy and a little spicy and definitely not your mother's breakfast grits. They will continue to cook as they sit, so make them nice and loose so they don't get too thick at the table.

In a medium saucepan over medium heat, melt the butter. Add the jalapeños and garlic and cook, stirring often, for 2 minutes. Add 2 cups water, the milk, salt, and pepper. Bring to a simmer. Add the grits and mix well. Return to a simmer and cook until the grits are creamy and thick, 5 to 7 minutes. Add the cheese and mix well. Continue cooking and mixing until the cheese is fully incorporated. If the grits get too thick, add a little more milk to thin them out. Serve immediately.

¼ cup butter

2 jalapeños, seeded and minced (if you like it spicy, leave the seeds in)

2 garlic cloves, crushed

2 cups milk, plus more as needed

2 teaspoons salt

½ teaspoon black pepper

1 cup quick grits

2 cups grated sharp Cheddar cheese

CHEESY MAC AND CHEESE

MAKES
8
SERVINGS

1 pound uncooked elbow macaroni

4 tablespoons butter

2 cups half-and-half

8 ounces Velveeta, cut into 1-inch cubes

2 cups shredded sharp Cheddar cheese

2 cups shredded Jack cheese

1 teaspoon salt

½ teaspoon black pepper

½ cup panko bread crumbs

Everybody loves macaroni and cheese, and it goes very well with all kinds of barbecue. This is a very traditional version with elbow macaroni and a creamy and cheesy sauce. The secret ingredient is the Velveeta. Add a little cooked bacon for a real treat.

Cook the macaroni per the package instructions. Drain the macaroni, transfer it to a large bowl, and set aside.

Preheat the broiler on high.

In a large saucepan, melt 2 tablespoons of the butter over medium heat. Add the half-and-half and bring to a simmer. Add the Velveeta and continue cooking, stirring occasionally, until well blended. Add the Cheddar, Jack, salt, and pepper. Continue cooking, stirring often, until well blended. Pour the cheese mixture over the macaroni and mix well. Transfer the macaroni mixture to a greased 3-quart baking dish.

Put the bread crumbs in a small bowl. In another small bowl, melt the remaining 2 tablespoons butter in the microwave. Pour the butter over the bread crumbs and mix well. Spread the bread crumb mixture evenly over the casserole. Place the casserole under the broiler until golden brown, about 3 minutes. Serve immediately.

DR. BBQ'S BACON MAQUE CHOUX

MAKES
8
SERVINGS

Maque choux is a dish from south Louisiana and it's really not a traditional side for barbecue. But it's mostly bacon, corn, bell peppers, and (in my version) cheese, so it sure goes well with barbecue. I've been sneaking this one in on the barbecue table for years and nobody has complained yet.

In a Dutch oven over medium heat, cook the bacon until it is just starting to crisp. Add the butter, onion, celery, bell peppers, chiles, and garlic. Mix well and cook, stirring occasionally, until the onion is soft, about 10 minutes. Add the corn, flour, Creole seasoning, sugar, pepper, and thyme. Mix well. Cover and cook over low heat for 10 minutes, until the corn is tender. Add the tomatoes and cheese and mix well. Continue cooking and mixing until the cheese is melted and fully incorporated. Pour the maque choux into a bowl and garnish with green onions before serving.

8 ounces bacon, diced

2 tablespoons butter

1 cup finely diced onion

½ cup finely diced celery

½ cup finely diced green bell pepper

½ cup finely diced red bell pepper

2 serrano chiles, seeded and minced

3 garlic cloves, crushed

Three 11-ounce cans niblet corn, drained

2 tablespoons flour

1 tablespoon Creole seasoning

1 teaspoon Sugar in the Raw

½ teaspoon black pepper

½ teaspoon dried thyme

One 10-ounce can diced tomatoes with green chiles

8 ounces Velveeta, cut into 1-inch cubes

Sliced green onions

MARSHA'S CHOCOLATE BUTTERMILK MAC PIE

MAKES
6
SERVINGS

CRUST

½ cup finely chopped
macadamia nuts

1 cup all-purpose flour

⅓ cup butter

1 egg, beaten

FILLING

1¼ cups sugar

3 tablespoons cornmeal

3 eggs, beaten

½ cup butter, melted

⅓ cup buttermilk

1 teaspoon vanilla extract

2 tablespoons cocoa powder

My friend Marsha Hale from Lynchburg, Tennessee, is a real Southern cook and a real barbecue girl. I always include a recipe from Marsha in my books and she always comes up with something great for me. Buttermilk pie is definitely a necessary side for barbecue, but for this book Marsha made me a very special version with cocoa and macadamia nuts.

Preheat the oven to 350°F.

To make the crust: Place the chopped nuts on a sheet pan and toast, stirring occasionally, until golden, 5 to 10 minutes. Transfer them to a plate to cool. Leave the oven on.

In a medium bowl, combine the flour and toasted nuts. Cut in the butter with a pastry blender or two knives until the mixture forms coarse crumbs. Add the egg and 1 teaspoon cold water and mix until combined. With your hands, form the dough into a ball. Wrap tightly in plastic wrap and refrigerate for at least 30 minutes (and up to 1 day).

Roll out the dough on a lightly floured surface until it's big enough to fit a 9-inch pie plate. Lay the dough on the pie plate and ease it into the corners. Fold the edges under and flute them.

To make the filling: In a medium bowl, combine the sugar and cornmeal. Add the eggs, butter, buttermilk, and vanilla. Using an electric hand mixer on medium speed, mix until well blended, about 2 minutes. Add the cocoa powder and mix until well blended, about I minute.

Pour the mixture into the pie crust, spreading it evenly. Bake for about 45 minutes, until the center is set. Transfer the pie to a wire rack to cool for I hour before serving.

THE WORLD'S GREATEST BANANA PUDDING

MAKES ABOUT
10
SERVINGS

This really is the best banana pudding I've ever eaten. It's simple and the ingredients are pretty common, but some things are just best when made the old-fashioned way. Make sure you use ripe bananas and as many vanilla wafers as you need to cover the bottom of your pan.

In a large bowl, combine the instant pudding with the milk. Whisk them together until smooth. Add the sweetened condensed milk and vanilla and mix well. Add the whipped topping and mix well.

Line the bottom of a 9-by-13-inch baking dish with half the vanilla wafers. Top with the sliced bananas. Mix the pudding again and then pour it over the bananas, spreading it evenly. Top with the rest of the vanilla wafers, making a nice design if you like. Cover with plastic wrap and refrigerate for 1 hour, so the pudding becomes firm, before serving.

One 5-ounce box instant vanilla pudding

3 cups whole milk

One 14-ounce can sweetened condensed milk

1 teaspoon vanilla extract

One 8-ounce tub whipped topping

60 vanilla wafers (use more or less if you like)

5 bananas, peeled and sliced ½ inch thick

INDEX

TABLE OF EQUIVALENTS

The exact equivalents in the following tables have been rounded for convenience.

Liquid/Dry Measurements

U.S.	Metric
¼ teaspoon	1.25 milliliters
½ teaspoon	2.5 milliliters
1 teaspoon	5 milliliters
1 tablespoon (3 teaspoons)	15 milliliters
1 fluid ounce (2 tablespoons)	30 milliliters
¼ cup	60 milliliters
⅓ cup	80 milliliters
½ cup	120 milliliters
1 cup	240 milliliters
1 pint (2 cups)	480 milliliters
1 quart (4 cups, 32 ounces)	960 milliliters
1 gallon (4 quarts)	3.84 liters
1 ounce (by weight)	28 grams
1 pound	448 grams
2.2 pounds	1 kilogram

Lengths

U.S.	Metric
⅛ inch	3 millimeters
¼ inch	6 millimeters
½ inch	12 millimeters
1 inch	2.5 centimeters

Oven Temperature

Fahrenheit	Celsius	Gas
250	120	½
275	140	1
300	150	2
325	160	3
350	180	4
375	190	5
400	200	6
425	220	7
450	230	8
475	240	9
500	260	10